WHAT'S
YOUR GAME?

A RESOURCE BOOK FOR
MATHEMATICAL ACTIVITIES

Michael Cornelius
& Alan Parr

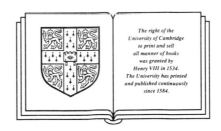

The right of the
University of Cambridge
to print and sell
all manner of books
was granted by
Henry VIII in 1534.
The University has printed
and published continuously
since 1584.

CAMBRIDGE UNIVERSITY PRESS
Cambridge
New York   Port Chester
Melbourne   Sydney

Published by the Press Syndicate of the University of Cambridge
The Pitt Building, Trumpington Street, Cambridge CB2 1RP
40 West 20th Street, New York, NY 10011–4211, USA
10 Stamford Road, Oakleigh, Melbourne 3166, Australia

© Cambridge University Press 1991
First published 1991
Printed in Great Britain by Scotprint Ltd, Musselburgh

British Library cataloguing-in-publication data

Cornelius, Michael
What's your game?
1. Schools. Curriculum subjects: Mathematics. Teaching
aids: Board games
I. Title   II. Parr, Alan
510.078
ISBN 0 521 38625 X

CONTENTS

The Authors

Michael Cornelius is Senior Lecturer in Mathematical Education at the University of Durham. He previously taught in schools in Hertfordshire, Merseyside and Somerset. He is co-author (with Robbie Bell) of *Board Games Round the World* and is Editor-in-Chief of the Mathematical Association.

Alan Parr is Mathematics Adviser for Hertfordshire. He taught in Nottinghamshire and Buckinghamshire before moving to Hertfordshire as teacher and subsequently Advisory Teacher. He is the author of *Take Ten Cards* (Egon Publications) and has published more than one hundred issues of his own games magazine, *Hopscotch*.

Acknowledgements

Many teachers and pupils have helped in trying out some of the games in this book. Particular thanks are due to staff and pupils at:

Park View Comprehensive School, Chester-le-Street,
Ralph Sadleir Middle School, Puckeridge
St Bede's R.C. Comprehensive School, Peterlee,
Wolsingham Comprehensive School, Co. Durham

and to:

Maureen Defty, Charlotte Gould, Marie Peat, Bill Polley, Teun Spaans and Mike Taylor; many games inventors who gave permission to use their ideas; and a vast number of friends (both children and adults) who shared in the development of many of the games.

The following games manufacturers kindly supplied information:

Hiron Games and Maureen Hiron, London
Invicta Plastics Limited, Leicester
Paradigm Games Limited, London
Red Dragon Games Limited, Pembroke Dock

Thanks are also due to Rosemary Tennison at the Cambridge University Press for her interest and assistance and to Ray Kitching who helped with the photographs.

1 INTRODUCTION

Games provide a source of enjoyment, interest and fascination for many people. This book seeks to offer a variety of games which could be played by children (and adults) from a wide range of ages and which might lead to some investigation of possibilities and strategies. Although the material included is aimed primarily at the teacher of mathematics and his or her pupils, most of the games should have a much wider appeal. The authors' starting point was to produce a resource book for mathematical investigations which would serve as a companion volume to *Board Games Round the World*, Bell and Cornelius (1988), but would include both known and unknown 'modern' games.

Some of the games included will be well known, others will be new to readers. Some games are available commercially, others have never been publicly produced. In deciding what to include, the chief criterion for selection has been 'simplicity', in order for a teacher to be able to make easy use of a game it should require minimal equipment, and that equipment should be readily obtainable at minimum cost. It is better (and more fun) for pupils to make their own playing materials than for teachers to purchase expensive, commercially-produced products.

In putting together this collection of games we have been conscious of the difficulty of *classification*. Having started with categories such as 'Pencil and Paper Games', 'Card Games' and 'Board Games' we finally decided on categories which would give the reader both a rough indication of the *content* of a game (e.g. *number* or *geometry*) and a guide to *materials needed* (e.g. *pencil and paper* or *cards*). We would, however, urge the reader and user of this book not to become too concerned with problems of classification as most games could easily be moved from one category to another and many could appear in more than one section.

The core of the book consists of six chapters describing various games: each game is followed by a series of suggestions for investigations/activities which might arise from it. Comments on some of these investigations are given in chapter 10. The majority of the activities suggested have been tried out in school classrooms and chapter 8 offers some comments on the use of games in school mathematics together with discussion of pupils' reactions. Every lesson is unique and its success or failure depends on a large number of factors, most importantly the relationship between the teacher and pupils. As all teachers will know, an activity which works well on one occasion may well prove a disaster on another for no apparent reason.

For schools in England and Wales, the introduction of the National Curriculum, HMSO (1989) is an event of massive significance. It will be a number of years before the full implications of this curriculum and the assessment procedures associated with it are fully apparent but it seemed sensible, in a book such as this, to offer some indication of levels for which suggested activities might be suitable. Thus chapter 9 provides a list of games and suggestions of National Curriculum 'Key Stages' and 'Attainment Targets' for which they might provide suitable enrichment material. It is extremely unlikely that any two people would reach complete agreement on the exact areas where a game might be useful and so the list should be taken as no more than a very rough guide. However it may help the busy teacher looking for ideas to use in a particular area. One thing which does emerge from the listing is the wide use possible for many games: in testing material in schools some games produced interest in age groups ranging from seven-year-olds to eighteen-year-olds. The National Curriculum should allow scope for flexibility and originality: we believe that the investigations we suggest will enable the teacher to provide work which is directly relevant to the curriculum and which will, at the same time, appear as something different from normal mathematics.

One of the early criticisms of the National Curriculum centred on the problem of 'cross-curricular' activity. It was therefore encouraging to see much emphasis put on this aspect in *Mathematics: Non-Statutory Guidance*, National Curriculum Council (1989), issued as a supplement to the National Curriculum. Games can provide a superb motivation for cross-curricular activity. In addition to the mathematics which might be extracted from games, we suggest:

(i) practical work in art/design etc. in making equipment for games,
(ii) oral and written work in discussing and describing games (for example, writing a set of rules for a game, however simple, is a first class language activity),
(iii) physical activity in which the 'playing' pieces are real people.
(iv) background work on the geographical/historical origins of games,
(v) computer programming and its use in the analysis of games.

The reader will undoubtedly think of many other possibilities but additionally playing games is an important form of social intercourse and, if children have not experienced such activities in their home life, it is all the more important that school should give them the chance to play. Playing a game offers the experience of losing (and winning) with grace and at the same time the chance to play in a spirit of cooperation, for mutual enjoyment, rather than with the sole aim of winning at all costs.

Computer implementations of many of the games featured in this book are readily available, particularly with BBC series machines. The solitary games player will find a machine an ever-willing opponent but the playing of games is essentially a social activity and care should be taken not to over-use the scarce resources of the computer when actual pupil-pupil contact is likely to be more fun and to produce better and more active learning.

Perhaps the most common use of a game in the mathematics classroom, whether or not a computer is involved, is to give pupils some enjoyable practice in arithmetical skills. Whilst not decrying this use, it has been our aim throughout this book to draw attention to the fact that most games have all sorts of questions inside them just waiting to be brought out:

How many moves are possible?

What is the biggest score I can make?

How many squares are within range of this piece?

How many combinations of numbers can I make with two cards?

and so on ...

Although such questions may be drawn out of almost any game, it is undeniable that many games players play at a superficial level and never consciously think in these terms. However a game against a computer makes it particularly easy for a teacher to raise such issues. It is usually simple to connect up a television to give an additional screen display so that everyone, even in a large class, can see what is going on and so a game can be quickly introduced to an entire class and particular situations can be readily illustrated.

Children appreciate both a computer's neutrality (it does not pour scorn on even the most unconsidered comment) and its infinite patience. The computer can operate equally well in two modes: as the neutral recorder of a game between players, or as the opponent of a pupil (or team of pupils). Further, it is accurate and reliable: how many games of *Mastermind* have been ruined because the passive player became bored and assessed enquiries carelessly? In games like *Mastermind* or *Lap* (chapter 7) it is more fun to be the active player making the observations and deductions than it is to be the one doing the setting and assessing: with a computer version you can be the active player for as long as you wish and you can be sure that the computer will not get bored and mark your guesses inaccurately.

Some of the games in this book exist in computer versions, e.g. 'Pig', '31', '37' and '57' in chapter 2 or 'Elephant' and 'Rhino' in chapter 7, details of sources for these games appear at the end of the book. Computer versions of other games will often be found in monthly computer magazines or informally produced collections. Sometimes the computer adds little: there is not much to be gained from playing an inflexible and poorly-programmed version of *Noughts and Crosses* when more can be gained from a real game. Still more limited are various drill and practice 'games' in which children are invited to manipulate numbers in a totally meaningless context. The main value of the computer lies in its ability to stimulate the imagination: often ten minutes work at a keyboard can develop into hours of quality work away from the computer.

It is no good having a game which is not *played!* Thus we believe it is vital for pupils to play the games described before considering activities/investigations which might arise, through playing will come familiarity and through familiarity will come a much better feel for a game and for activities associated with it. In the preparation of this book we wrote to a number of games manufacturers: in a footnote to a reply about Quadromania (see chapter 6) one of the directors of Red Dragon Games, John Lloyd, wrote:

'I hope that whatever you write will not overdo the educational aspect: the game is above all enjoyable to play. As one who has spent his life resisting what people tell me is good for me, I would run a mile if I thought Quadromania was for swots!'

We strongly endorse this comment.

Playing games is fun for most people. We think that doing mathematics should be fun. If this book helps teachers to make pupils see that there is fun in both games and mathematics, the authors will feel that they have achieved something of value. At the same time we hope that many readers will find interest in playing the games without worrying about the mathematics!

2 NUMBER GAMES WITH COUNTERS, MATCHSTICKS AND DICE

The use of simple equipment can often make a game more appealing and attractive: this chapter includes games which use readily obtainable objects such as matchsticks, counters or dice. In many instances the games could easily be played with pencil and paper alone but there is more fun to be had in using physical objects and indeed classroom use shows that pupils display far greater interest and make far greater progress with a game if some simple 'apparatus' is involved. The effort needed to organise a game with some practical equipment is amply rewarded by the subsequent increased interest; it is worth settling for a 'messy' (perhaps noisy) classroom in return for worthwhile, enthusiastic activity. There is another factor, 'tactility'. Playing chess with a good quality set of wooden pieces is vastly more enjoyable than a game with cheap plastic ones. In the same way, playing games with good 'chunky' counters which you can fidget with is better than using an assortment of buttons and tiddleywinks. Watch adults, and children, play a game and notice how fiddling with pieces seems to encourage thinking!

2.1 Westbury

The name of this game comes from the inventors, a class of ten-year-old pupils at Westbury JMI school in Hertfordshire. It illustrates one of many possibilities using matchsticks to represent numbers in the style used on calculators, digital clocks, etc.

Figure 2.1

The game needs a supply of matchsticks (preferably with heads removed), cocktail sticks or something similar: 'lolly' sticks which can be bought by the thousand offer an excellent

9

resource here. All calculator manufacturers seem to have settled on a standard seven segment display for representing digits as in figure 2.1.

However it is worth noting that digital displays elsewhere, for example on video recorders, digital watches and clocks and outside petrol stations, often vary the form of some digits so that, for example, 'seven' might appear without the 'tail' on the top left hand side. The game begins with the number 88 being set up with 14 matchsticks. Two players now take turns to move any *two* sticks to make a bigger number, for example

showing player 1 changing 88 to 100 and then player 2 changing 100 to 196. Play continues until a player is unable to play and the last player able to make a legal move is the winner.

As a variation the rules can be changed to allow *either* repositioning of two sticks *or* the complete removal of two.

Investigations

(i)   What numbers can be made from exactly 14 sticks?
Which of these numbers cannot be attained in the game?
What is the highest number possible?
Can you find a sequence starting at 88 by which this highest number can be reached in actual play?

(ii) Suppose the game with 14 sticks is limited to two/three digit numbers, what is the highest number possible? From which numbers can it be reached?

(iii) Investigate 'Westbury' with different starting numbers, for example 89, 90 or 91.

(iv) What numbers can be made with exactly ten sticks?

2.2 Grundy's Game

Originally known as *Distich*, the exact origin of this game is unknown. It is played by two players with an agreed number of counters arranged in piles. The players move alternately and, on each turn, may divide any pile into two *unequal* piles, thus, for example, a pile of 6 could be divided into piles of 5 and 1 or 4 and 2 but *not* 3 and 3. Piles containing 1 or 2 counters are thus unplayable. The winner is the last player able to make a legal move. It is probably best to begin playing the game with a *single* pile. A game beginning with 11 counters might go as follows:

	11						
A leaves:	9	2					
B leaves:	6	3	2				
A leaves:	5	1	3	2			
B leaves:	3	2	1	3	2		
A leaves:	2	1	2	1	3	2	
B leaves:	2	1	2	1	2	1	2

and B wins since A cannot now move.

Grundy's game in progress

Investigations

(i)   For games starting with a single pile, investigate which player should win if you begin with 3, 4, 5, ... counters?
How many moves are possible in each game?

(ii) Is it possible to predict the winner of a game starting with any number of counters?

(iii) Consider a variation in which piles can be *only* divided into any number of *equal* piles (not 1s). For example, 12 could be divided to give 6+6, 4+4+4, 3+3+3+3 or 2+2+2+2+2+2 but 11 could not be divided. Investigate what happens and try to discover winning strategies for given starting numbers.

2.3 Fair Shares and Varied Pairs

This game was invented by John Conway who also invented *Sprouts* (see chapter 5). It has close links with Grundy's Game. Two players set out counters in piles and, playing alternately, at a turn a player can either:

split any pile into equal, smaller piles, for example, 6 into 3+3, 2+2+2 or 1+1+1+1+1+1,

or combine two unequal piles to make a larger pile. The winner is the last person to be able to make one of these moves.

Here are two examples of games:

(i) start with	3	2			
A leaves:	3	1	1		
B leaves:	1	1	1	1	1

and wins;

(ii) start with	5	4	
A leaves:	5	2	2
B leaves:	7	2	
A leaves:	7	1	1

and B wins on the next move by splitting the 7 into 1s.

Investigations

(i) In a game using 5 counters, find all the possible starting combinations and investigate which player should win.

(ii) What happens if you start with 1, 2, 3, 4, 5, ... counters?

(iii) Is it possible for a draw to be achieved?

2.4 Pig

Pig is simple and exciting! It has been around for a long time although its exact origin is not known. The game has immense value and potential for teaching at all levels: at its simplest level it offers good practice in rapid mental addition.

One ordinary die is needed and any number of players can take part although four is a convenient maximum. In turn players throw the die as many times as they wish, keeping a record of the total of the numbers thrown. At any stage the turn may be ended and the player *banks* the total scored, adding it to any earlier score achieved. However if a 1 is thrown all the player's score for the turn is lost and the turn ends. The game is won by the first player to score 100 points or more. Thus, for example, a game between three players might have reached a stage where A has 62 points, B has 45 points and C has 10 points.

A throws 2, 6, 5 and stops, adding 13 to 62 to make 75;
B throws a 1 and score stays on 45;
C throws 6, 4, 6, 3, 1 and score stays on 10;
A throws 6, 3, 2, 5, 4, 6 and wins since the score is now over 100.

The game of *Pig* has been used enthusiastically by teachers in data collection and data handling activities: see also the note on the game *Digame* in chapter 9.

In 1984 a commercial version called *Pass the Pigs* (MB Games) appeared; if the reader has never tried this game then he or she should try it as soon as possible, it is even more fun than *Pig* itself!

The game of 'Pass the Pigs'

Instead of a die the player throws two plastic pigs which can fall in a number of orientations (for example, on feet, on back, on snout) and scores are made accordingly. The game has potential for the mathematics classroom in view of the use of a 'non–standard' die (i.e. the pig) with different probabilities for the various possible outcomes. *Pass the Pigs* is eminently suitable for very young children: the only scores possible are either 1 or multiples of 5 or 10. A set would be useful in every infant classroom!

Investigations

(i)   Throw a die a large number of times. What is the typical length of a chain before a '1' appears?
      What is the longest chain made up entirely of '1s'?

(ii) In the light of data collected in (i) suggest the best tactics for 'Pig'. For example, one theory suggests that you should keep throwing until you have reached a score of 13 or more and then stick.

(iii) How do things change if the 'losing' number is a '6' instead of a '1'?

(iv) Investigate games with other dice for example a '0 to 9' or a '1 to 10' die.

(v)   What is the probability of reaching 10 without throwing a '1'?

2.5 The Thirty-one Game

The origin of this game is *The Canterbury Puzzles* by Henry Dudeney (1847–1930), if the reader is unfamiliar with this book then he or she is strongly recommended to find a copy because it is full of imaginative ideas which can be used in classrooms.

Dudeney's original game was, he claimed, 'a favourite means of swindling employed by card-sharpers at racecourses and in railway carriages'. In his version 24 cards are laid down as in figure 2.4.

Two players take turns to turn a card face down, for example the first player turns over a '2' and counts 'two', then the second player turns over the '5' and counts 'seven', then the first player a '1' counting 'eight' and so on. A player wins if he

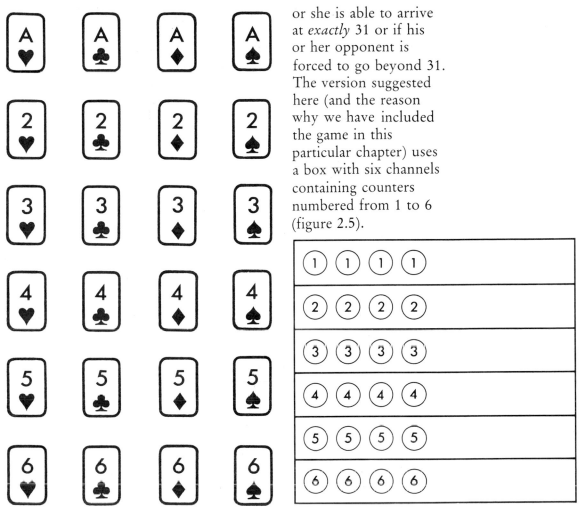

or she is able to arrive at *exactly* 31 or if his or her opponent is forced to go beyond 31. The version suggested here (and the reason why we have included the game in this particular chapter) uses a box with six channels containing counters numbered from 1 to 6 (figure 2.5).

Figure 2.4

Figure 2.5

As the game is played the counters can be moved across to the right, making it easy to keep track of which counters have been used and also making the cumulative score easier to keep. Otherwise the rules are the same as those for Dudeney's original game and a player wins with exactly opponent 31 or if the is forced past that number.

Investigations

(i) How many turns are there in (a) the shortest and (b) the longest games possible?

(ii) What number should the starting player take? Can that player ensure a win? If so, how?

(iii) Investigate the game with smaller sets of numbers and different targets.

(iv) (harder) How many ways are there of reaching 31?

2.6 The Thirty-seven Game

This is another game from Henry Dudeney (see Dudeney (1958)). The numbers 1, 2, 3, 4, 5 are written in a line as shown in figure 2.6:

Figure 2.6

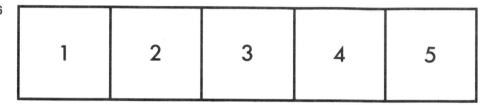

Player 1 places a coin on a top of one number, player 2 then moves the coin to another number and adds the numbers together, player 1 now moves the coin and adds the new number and so on. The object of the game is to score 37 *exactly* or to force your opponent beyond 37. Thus a game might begin:
Player 1: 5, Player 2: 2 (total 7), Player 1: 3 (total 10), Player 2: 5 (total 15) etc.

Investigations

(i) What is (a) the quickest and (b) the longest way in which 37 can be reached?

(ii) Can the first player develop a winning strategy?

(iii) Try the game with different target numbers.

2.7 The Fifty-seven Game

For obvious reasons this game is often referred to as *Heinz*. It was devised by Trevor Truran, a writer on games and puzzles (Truran (1984)).
A magic square is drawn as in figure 2.7.

Two players need a copy of this square and a coin or a counter. The first player places the coin on any square and counts the number as a starting total, the second player now moves the coin to a new square and adds the number to the total. *When moved, the counter must not be placed in the same row or column as the previous number.* So for example, if the first player puts the counter on '9', the second player cannot

6	7	2
1	5	9
8	3	4

Figure 2.7

3	2	1
2	1	3
1	3	2

Figure 2.8

use 1, 5, 2 or 4. If the second player chose '7', then the total would be 9+7=16 and so on. The game is won if a player reaches a score of exactly 57 or forces the opponent beyond that number.

Investigations

(i) How many squares can you move to from each square? What is the sum of their numbers in each case?

(ii) What are the shortest and longest possible games?

(iii) Try playing on a simpler board for example figure 2.8.

Try also different target numbers.

(iv) Investigate the *Fifty-seven Game* if the rules are changed so that you *must* play in either the same row or the same column as the previous move.

2.8 The Pentomino Game

This game is both simple and elegant. It uses the twelve 'pentominoes' i.e. the twelve shapes that can be made by joining five squares together (see figure 2.9).

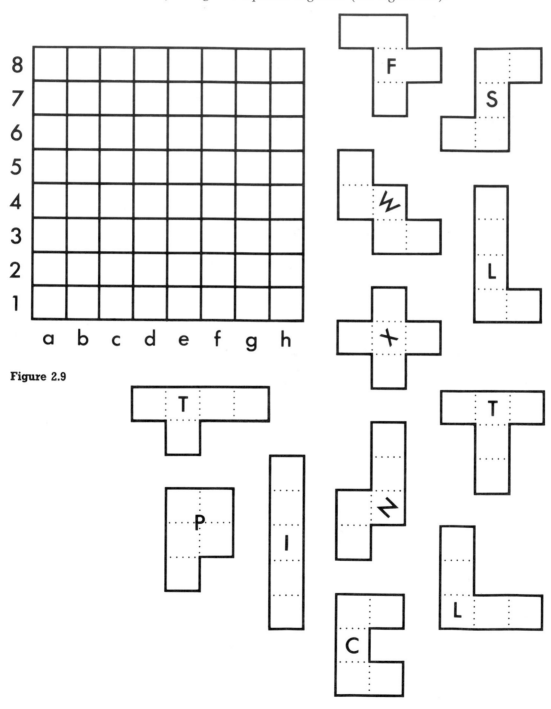

Figure 2.9

There is much fascinating work which can be done with pentominoes. The only 12 possible configurations for 5 squares joined by sides are as illustrated, it is a useful exercise to discover which of these can be folded to make a cubical box without a top. As an extension, 'hexominoes' (shapes made with 6 squares) can be investigated, some of these will fold into closed cubical boxes. For fuller details see for example Bolt (1982).

An 8×8 grid is also needed. Two players alternately place a chosen pentomino on the grid. Play continues until one player is unable to make a move and loses. Before the game is introduced, there is clearly scope for pupils to discover the twelve pentominoes, thereafter the game provides an actual use for the pentominoes which is better than sticking them on a sheet or throwing them away!

Investigations

(i)   Is it possible to position all twelve pentominoes on the board?

(ii) What is the smallest number of pieces that can be placed before a game ends?

(iii) Should the first player be able to force a win?

(iv) Find all possible 'triominoes' (shapes with 3 squares) and 'quadrominoes' (4 squares). Invent a game using these. What about a game using 'hexominoes'?

3 NUMBER GAMES WITH CARDS

To most people *cards* means a standard pack of 52 playing-cards divided into four suits: hearts, clubs, diamonds and spades. Although this chapter includes some games played with such a pack, there are also games played with much simpler sets of cards and the only equipment needed is often some blank pieces of card and a pen. It is possible to discover (and invent) very simple games using, for example, a set of cards numbered 0 to 9. At the same time games with standard playing cards should not be ignored as a source of ideas; there are many books describing such games, for example Waddington (1983).

Playing cards from Russia (top left, bottom right), France (top right) and Japan (bottom left)

3.1 The Sixteen Game (Seize)

Two players have one set of cards numbered 0 to 9 between them. The cards are placed face up on the table and, in turn, the players choose a card which is then kept face up in front of the person who chose it. The winner is the first player to have *three* cards which total exactly 16. (If the first three cards chosen do not add up to 16, the players continue to choose cards and try to get a set of three totalling 16 exactly.)

Investigations

(i) In how many ways can a total of 16 be made with three cards?

(ii) What is the greatest number of cards a player could have without holding a winning triplet?

(iii) Investigate different target numbers. How many ways are there of making other totals (for example 12, 13, 14, 15 ...) with three cards? Are there any patterns?

(iv) Investigate a multiplicative version using cards numbered 1 to 12 in which the winner is the first player to collect three cards with a *product* of 72 (say).

3.2 Nimble

This is a card version of the most elementary game in the *Nim* family.

One set of cards numbered 1 to 9 is placed face up and in order on a table. Two players, playing alternately, play according to the following rule:

> You must pick up the highest numbered card and you *may* pick up the second highest card as well (i.e. you must take either one or two cards).

The winner is the player who picks up the '1' card.

Investigations

(i) Who should win? How? Consider games with smaller and larger numbers of cards and try to find a pattern.

(ii) Suppose you play with a set of cards from 1 to 20. What are the winning positions?

(iii) Investigate a modified game where the rules stipulate that 1, 2 or 3 cards may be taken at a turn.

(iv) What are the smallest and largest total scores possible on the cards which can be held in the winner's hand?

3.3 Manifest

This game was invented by Frank Tapson who suggested the more prosaic title *Show Most, Take*.

Two (or more) players each start with a complete set of cards numbered 0 to 9. Play is in four 'rounds':

The end of a game of 'Manifest'

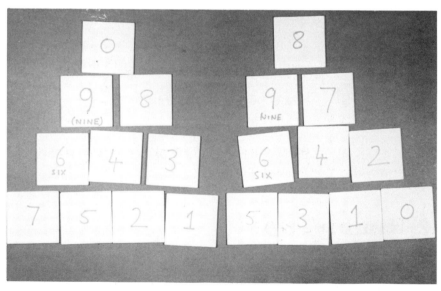

Round 1: Each player places one card face down. The cards are then turned over and the player showing the highest number wins one point. (If two or more players share the highest number, they each score a point.)

Round 2: Each player now places *two* cards face down, arranged to show the highest value (for example a 3

and a 6 would be used to show 63 and not 36).
When the cards are turned over the player with the highest number scores two points.

Round 3: Players now place *three* cards face down, arranging them to show the highest number. The winner scores three points.

Round 4: The players play their last four cards, again making the highest number possible. The winner scores four points.

The winner is the player with the greatest number of points or, alternatively, several games can be played with the winner being the first to an agreed target, for example 25 points.

Investigations

For a two player game:

(i) What final scores are possible? (Assume, initially, that no rounds result in a 'tie'.)
Can one player win all four rounds?

(ii) Investigate a game in which the lowest number of points wins.

(iii) Investigate an eight round game played with two sets of cards each and playing 1, 2, 3, 4, 1, 2, 3, 4 cards on successive rounds.

For a three player game:

(iv) Investigate a game where the final winner is the player with the *middle* number of points.

3.4 Ten or Twenty

This is similar to *Seize* (see page 20) and comes from Silverman (1971). It can be played with the cards from ace to 9 from a single suit of a pack of playing cards. Two players pick up a card alternately. The aim is to collect three cards which have a total of either 10 or 20. The ace counts as '1' only.

Investigations

(i) What winning combinations are possible?

(ii) What is (a) the best and (b) the worst card to select on the first move if you start?

(iii) Is a draw possible?

(iv) What is the greatest number of cards you can hold without having a winning combination?

3.5 The Fifteen Game

This game is based on a similar one in Silverman (1971). A set of cards numbered from 1 to 9 is needed and also a 3×3 square grid (figure 3.1).

Two players are needed. One has the five odd cards, the other the even. Starting with the player who has the odd cards, the players take turns to put a card on the grid. The game is won when one player completes a line (vertically, horizontally or diagonally) of three cards which add up to exactly 15. The three cards in the winning line need not all have been played by the same player.

A variation is to play the game with a set of ten cards either numbered from 0 to 9 or from 1 to 10.

Figure 3.1

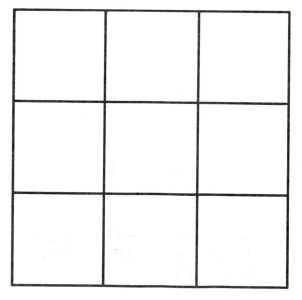

Investigations

(i) How many winning combinations (for example 4, 5, 6) are possible?

(ii)   Is a draw possible?

(iii) Can either player win using only his/her own cards?

(iv)   Investigate different winning targets for example 14 or 16.

3.6 Split

A set of cards numbered from 1 to 30 is needed for this
two-player game.

At the start the '30' card is placed face up in the centre of
the table with the other cards face up on one side. The first
player chooses two cards which add up to 30 (say, 13 and 17)
and uses them to replace the '30' card on the table. The second
player then chooses two cards to replace one of these (for
example the 13 might be replaced with 10 and 3). Play
continues until one player cannot make a move and loses.

So, a game might proceed:

30						
2	28					
2	3	25				
2	3	4	21			
2	3	4	5	16		
2	3	4	5	6	10	
2	3	4	5	6	9	1

and then no further split is possible.

Investigations

(i)   What are the shortest and longest games possible?

(ii)   Is there a best first move?

(iii) How many different games are possible: (a) if you use cards
       numbered 1 to 6, (b) with cards from 1 to 30? How many
       opening moves are possible in each case?

(iv)   Invent a game with the numbers from −15 to +15 with '15'
       being used to start. Investigate what happens.

3.7 Gops

This game appears in Pennycook (1973). Its origin is uncertain — it is thought to have been played in Cambridge in the 1930s but there are also suggestions that it is a game of Jewish origin which was played widely in Europe. An ordinary pack of playing cards is needed.

Two players each take a complete suit, for example one takes clubs and one takes diamonds, and a third suit, for example hearts, is shuffled and placed face down in a pile. The aim of the game is to win the hearts, the cards are given values from 1 (ace) to 13 (king) giving a total of 91 points available.

A heart is turned face up and the two players 'bid' for it by each selecting a card which they keep face down initially. When both cards are revealed, the player of the higher one wins the heart (ace counts as 1 again). If both players play cards of the same value, the next heart is turned up, both players bid again and the winner takes two hearts (if a further tie, the players now bid for three hearts and so on). If there is a tie in bidding for the *last* heart, then the winner of the previous heart takes the last one as well. The winner is the player holding the higher number of points in hearts — thus a total of at least 46 is needed to win.

As variations: (a) the hearts could be placed in a row, face up, at the start so that players know in advance in what order they will come,

(b) players could be given a fixed number of 'points' and allowed to use any number of these on an individual bid.

Investigations

(i)   Try a game with just six cards from each suit. In how many different orders can the hearts appear?
Is it possible for one player to win all the hearts?
What is the maximum/minimum score possible for each player?

(ii) Answer the problems in (i) for the thirteen card game and investigate other numbers from 1 to 13.

(iii) (harder) What is the probability of a game in which there is a tie on each of the thirteen turns?

3.8 Divide and Conquer

For this game which is for two players you need the cards of one suit excluding ace, jack and king. Each player is dealt five cards. One card is selected by each player and placed face down. When both cards are revealed the higher card wins *unless*:

the lower card is a factor of the higher one,

or the lower card is one less than the higher one.

Thus (e.g.) a '2' beats a queen (counts 12)

a '3' beats a '4'

a '5' beats a '2'.

The winner is the player who has most cards at the end: usually a game consists of several rounds. A convenient way of keeping track of the score is to turn cards already played so that the narrow side is towards you if you win and the longer side towards you if you lose (this is usually done in duplicate bridge). For example in the illustration player A has won with three of the five cards played: '3' beats 'Q' (3 is a factor of 12), '5' beats '6' (one less), '4' loses to '7', '9' beats '2' and '8' loses to '10'.

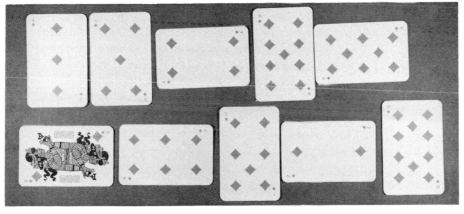

Divide and conquer – A game in progress

Investigations

(i)   Make up a table showing, for each card, which cards it beats and which cards it loses to.

(ii) How many different 'hands' are possible for a player?

(iii) Is it possible to have 2, 3, 4, 5 and 6 in the initial hand and win on all five plays?

(iv) Make up win/lose tables for different packs, use numbers up to 14, 15, 16, 17, 18. Is there any pattern?

3.9 The Dirty Dozen

There is the opportunity in this game to provide a lot of fun and hilarity in addition to some useful thinking about number operations. Any number of players from four to eight can play. Each player has a set of cards numbered from 1 to 12. Also needed are two further sets, one 'red' and the other 'blue'. The 'blue' cards have on them '+10', '+10', '+20', '+20', '+30', '−10', '−20', '−30', 'double your score', 'halve your score', 'divide your score by 3' and 'change sign'. The 'red' cards have 'highest' (3 cards), 'lowest' (3 cards), 'highest-giveaway' (2 cards), 'lowest-giveaway' (2 cards), 'second highest' (1 card) and 'second lowest' (1 card).

There are twelve rounds of play and each round starts with a red card and a blue card being turned face up, for example the blue card might be '+20' and the red card 'lowest'. Each player selects one card from his/her hand and puts it face down. When everyone has played, the cards are turned over and the '+20' card is won by the player who played the lowest *non-duplicated* card. The next pair of blue/red cards might be 'highest-giveaway' and '−10'; here the player of the highest *non-duplicated* card can give away the '−10' card to any chosen player. The 'change sign' card is obviously a good one to win if your score is highly negative but it can be helpful, and amusing, to pass it to whoever is winning! A 'double your score' card is not welcome if you have a score like −20!

Each player starts with a score of 20 and the game is won by the first player to reach, or pass, 100. No cards can be played twice from the same hand and any scores, at any stage in the game, which are not whole numbers are rounded up.

A game can finish very quickly but will often take a long time. After 12 rounds have been played, each player retrieves his/her cards and the blue and red packs are shuffled and replaced. An alternative game lasts for a fixed number of deals with the winner being the player with the highest score.

Investigations

(i)   What is the quickest route from 20 to 100 or from −50 to 100?

(ii) How many routes can you find which take you from 0 to 40 in three rounds?

(iii) Can you find scores from which you would reach the same new score whether you won: the 'double' or the '+30', or the 'change sign' and the '+20'?

4 NUMBER GAMES WITH PENCIL AND PAPER

Numbers have a fascination which can stir and occupy the minds of many people. Games with numbers can provide not only fun and amusement but they can also improve facility with mental arithmetic and basic number operations. The games in this chapter need no equipment other than pencil and paper and thus could be played in the classroom, at home, on a train, in an airport lounge . . . It is possible to overdo the 'games' aspect; after a children's party at which a parent had decided that number games (of the pencil and paper variety) were more fun than the traditional *Pass the Parcel* etc, the parent commented:

> 'Isn't it great, the children actually enjoyed playing games with numbers!'

whilst a child arriving home from the party said:

> 'Ugh! What a horrible party, we all had to do sums!'

4.1 Subtract a Square

This game comes from Silverman (1971). The game starts with a given number, say 42, and players alternately subtract a square number with the winner being the first to reach zero. Thus a sequence might be: 42 subtract 9, 33 subtract 4, 29 subtract 16, 13 subtract 1, 12 subtract 4, 8 subtract 1, 7 subtract 4, 3 subtract 1, 2 subtract 1, 1 subtract 1, 0.

The game offers an allied geometrical possibility, a rectangular grid of 42 squares could be shaded in as 'squares' are successively removed (see investigations).

Investigations

(i) Starting with 43, should the first player win?
What is the best starting move?

(ii) What is the smallest number of moves possible for starting numbers 1, 2, ..., 50?

(iii) What arrangements of squares can a given rectangle be divided into? For example a 3×5 rectangle:

Figure 4.1

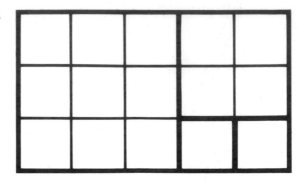

can be divided into a 3×3 square, a 2×2 square and two 1×1 squares.

(iv)   Investigate the hypothesis that any whole number can be written as the sum of not more than four squares.

4.2 Double or Take

This game is an extended form of 'Subtract a Square'. Two players are needed. Player A selects any number and player B can either double it or subtract any square or cube number. The aim of the game is to reach zero. So, for example, if A selects 73, then B can either double to 146 or subtract 1, 4, 8, 9, 16, 25, 27, 36, 49, or 64. Clearly (for example) subtraction of 9 or 64 would lose the game for B immediately. Rather the game might run as follows

A: 73   B: 24 (subtract 49)
A: 15 (subtract 9)   B: 30 (double)
A: 5 (subtract 25)   B: 10 (double)
A: 2 (subtract 8)

and B has now lost since the '2' can only be doubled to '4' (a square) or have '1' subtracted to leave '1' (a square and a cube).

The game provides an ideal opportunity to practise some arithmetic with squares and cubes and the rules can easily be modified to provide practice in other aspects of number.

Investigations

(i)   For the starting numbers from 1 to 10 work out which player should win: for example if A chooses '1', B wins immediately, if A chooses '2' then A will win, etc.

(ii) Which numbers from 1 to 100 will give (a) a win on the next move (for example 64) and (b) a win after two moves (for example 2)?

(iii) Investigate a game which allows only doubling the previous number or subtracting a prime number.

4.3 Number Squares

The game is played by two people on a 4×4 grid with the numbers 1, 2, 3, 4, 5, 6, 7, 8, 9, 10, 11, 12, 13, 14, 15, 16 underneath.

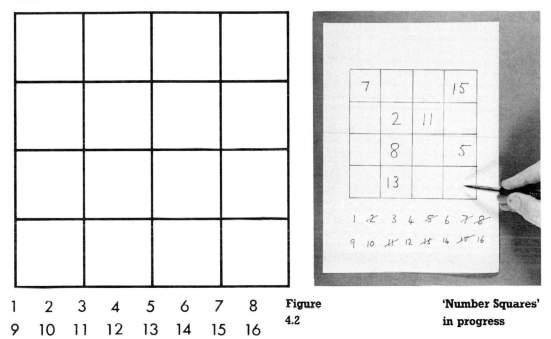

1 2 3 4 5 6 7 8
9 10 11 12 13 14 15 16

Figure 4.2

'Number Squares' in progress

The players play alternately and, at a turn, cross off one of the numbers and enter it on the grid. A player must not enter a number which leaves two consecutive numbers adjacent (either vertically, horizontally or diagonally). A player loses when unable to make a move.

Investigations

(i) Is a draw possible?
If so, in how many ways?

(ii) Investigate the game on a 3×3 grid with the numbers 1 to 9.

(iii) Investigate the game on a 4×4 grid with two sets of the numbers 1–8 (one set for each player).

(iv) Investigate a game on a hexagonal board (see figure 4.3) with the numbers 1 to 15. (The hexagonal board avoids any possible ambiguity about the meaning of 'adjacent'.)

Figure 4.3

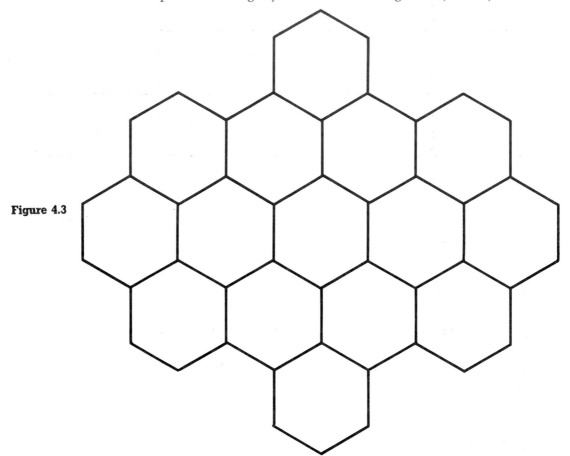

4.4 Difference

Two players play this game on a 4×4 grid with the numbers 1 to 8 written out twice underneath (figure 4.4).

Playing alternately, the players enter any number from the two rows on the grid (crossing off the number as they do so). When all the numbers have been used all the rows and columns are totalled. The first player scores the difference between the highest and lowest of the rows and the second player the difference between the highest and lowest of the columns. Figure 4.5 illustrates a score of 3 for the 'row' player and 2 for the 'column' player.

2	4	6	5	17
6	1	3	8	18
8	5	3	1	17
2	7	7	4	20
18	17	19	18	

1 2 3 4 5 6 7 8
1 2 3 4 5 6 7 8

Figure 4.4   **Figure 4.5**

Investigations

(i)   What are the maximum and minimum scores possible?
      Is a draw possible?

(ii) Try the game on other size grids for example 3×3, 5×5, 6×6.

(iii) Investigate the game with a single set of numbers from 1 to
      16 (instead of two sets from 1 to 8).

4.5 Undercut

This game has its origins in Douglas Hofstadter's column in
Scientific American. It involves a facility to bluff as well as a
facility with numbers!

Two players, A and B, each choose a whole number in the
range 1 to 5 and then compare choices. Each player scores
his/her number and adds it to his/her cumulative total *unless*
the players' chosen numbers differ by 1 in which case the
player of the lower number scores the sum of the two numbers
played and the player of the higher number scores nothing.
Thus a game might begin:
A plays 5, B plays 3 – A scores 5, B scores 3;
A plays 5, B plays 4 – A scores 0, B scores 9;
A plays 2, B plays 2 – A scores 2, B scores 2.

So, after three rounds, A has scored 7 and B has scored 14.

The winner is the first to reach, or exceed, an agreed target (for example 25).

A possible variation would be for each of the players to have five cards numbered 1 to 5, to play one at a time until all five have been played, then collect them together and start again.

Investigations

(i)   How many possible ways are there for the two players to choose the numbers?

(ii) With 25 as a target, what is the quickest game possible? What is the longest?

(iii) Investigate the game for different ranges of numbers for example 1 to 4, 1 to 6, etc.

4.6 Division Nim

Two players each write down an even number, these numbers are added to give a starting number for the game. In turn each player divides the last number obtained by one of its divisors (excluding '1'). The first player to reach '1' is the *loser*. Thus a game might run as follows:

A chooses 8, B chooses 16 so the game starts with 24.
A divides by 2   12
B divides by 3   4
A divides by 2   2
B divides by 2   1 (and B loses).

Investigations

(i)   For the numbers from 4 to 40, make a list of those with 2, 3, 4, 5, 6, . . . divisors. Does the list help you decide which player should win for a given starting number?

(ii) How many different games are possible starting with 36? Try other numbers. Is there a pattern?

(iii) Investigate what happens if, at the start, (a) both players choose odd numbers (b) one chooses odd and the other even.

4.7 Takeaway

The numbers 1 to 16 are placed at random in the squares of a 4×4 grid. For an example see figure 4.6.

Two players take turns to cross off a number and write it on a sheet in front of him/her. After the first number is crossed off a player must select a number which is in either the same row or the same column as the previous number chosen. Each player adds up the numbers on his/her sheet at the end of the game and the player with the higher total is the winner. Using the numbers in figure 4.6, a game might proceed:

A takes 16	B takes 13
A takes 9	B takes 10
A takes 11	B takes 15 ... and so on.

A game might end prematurely if either (a) all the numbers left in the array are inaccessible or (b) one player has achieved such a score that he/she cannot be caught. The game could also be played with *cards*, a pack numbered 1 to 16 could be shuffled and placed on the grid and players could physically remove the cards at each turn.

Figure 4.6

12	8	14	2
5	1	15	6
16	13	4	9
3	7	11	10

Investigations

(i) What is the quickest way in which one player could accumulate a winning score?

(ii) Is a draw possible?
      If it is, how and in how many ways?

(iii) Investigate the game for different sizes of grids.

(iv) What is the largest number of numbers which could be left
      inaccessible?
      What is the smallest possible winning score?

5 GEOMETRICAL GAMES WITH PENCIL AND PAPER

The games in this chapter are probably some of the simplest in the book yet many of them have an elegance which is appealing to pupils. All pose a challenge and usually there is immense satisfaction in discovering the structure of a game and in finding out how to outwit an opponent. In the classroom (see also chapter 8) these games proved to be some of the most popular with *Sim* and *Brussels Sprouts*, in particular, frequently clear favourites with all ages and all abilities. For those who doubt the value of games in the teaching of mathematics and who have as their main concern the achieving of high marks on external examinations, it is interesting to note a GCSE examination question from Summer, 1989. The Southern Examination Group on its Paper 3 (levels 2 and 3) set a question about a gardener putting string between stakes, the question was almost exactly the same as an analysis suggested by the game of *Sim*. Pupils, who a few weeks earlier had been introduced to *Sim*, were delighted to find that a question on an external examination paper suddenly became easy because they had investigated a game. Indeed they found it hard to believe that their teachers did not have second sight!

5.1 Three in a Row

This game is based on a suggestion in Averbach and Chein (1980). Fifteen dots are placed in a line as in figure 5.1.

• • • • • • • • • • • • • • •

Figure 5.1

Playing alternately, two players put a cross on any vacant dot. The winner is the first player to complete a row of three adjacent crosses anywhere along the line (the crosses do not all have to be made by the winning player).

It might be more fun to play the game with a marked out board (with fifteen squares in a row) and a set of counters, with one counter being placed on a square at each turn.

Investigations

(i) Who should win, the first or second player?

(ii)   Experiment with different numbers of dots (try 4,5,6 ...).
Can you explain what happens and who should win?

(iii) What happens if the number of adjacent dots needed to win
is different (for example 4)?

5.2 Sim

The game takes its name from its inventor, Gustavus J.
Simmons, a physicist in Albuquerque who invented it whilst
working on his Ph.D. on graph theory. He was not the first to
think of it but he was the first to try an extensive analysis, see
Simmons (1969) and Gardner (1973) for more detail. There is a
computer verison of the game using a nine-point polygon,
which is available as part of the MEP collection *Problem
solving and investigation*, it has been given the name *Ramsey*.

The beauty of the game lies in its simplicity and the fact
that a result is always obtained. In playing the game a draw has
never been achieved although we have not been able to
discover a proof that a draw is actually impossible. Six dots are
marked on a piece of paper in the form of a hexagon (figure 5.2).

Figure 5.2

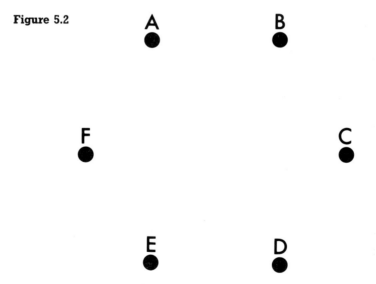

Two players play alternately. At a turn a player joins two
points with a straight line, each player using a different colour
(or, if using the same colour, one uses a dotted line). The aim
is to force an opponent to complete a triangle of his/her own
colour, the vertices of the triangle must be three of the points
A,B,C,D,E,F (triangles formed by crossing lines *within* the

hexagon do not count). Figure 5.3 shows a game in which Player 1 (full lines) has made six moves as has Player 2 (dotted lines). If Player 1 now chooses to draw AF then Player 2 is forced to draw either AB (and lose by completing triangle ADB and triangle ABC) or FE (and lose by completing triangle FDE).

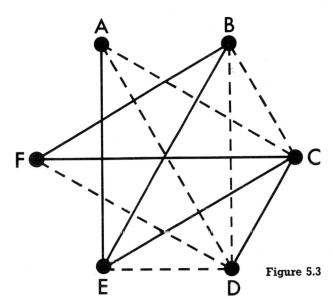

Figure 5.3

Children playing 'SIM'

Investigations

(i) What would happen if the game was played with:
(a) a set of four points forming a square,
(b) a set of five points forming a pentagon?

(ii) How many possible lines can be drawn in each of the square, pentagonal and hexagonal games?

(iii) How many different triangles can be made in a game of *Sim*? How many are equilateral, isosceles, right-angled?

(iv) How many different opening moves are possible? Is there a 'best' opening move?

(v) Can either player develop a winning strategy in either the original game or any of the simplified games?

(vi) Investigate larger games (for example with an octagon).

5.3 Hip

Hip could be regarded equally as a board game or as a pencil and paper one. If it is played with a pencil and paper then the array of dots in figure 5.4(a) can be used. If it is played as a board game then either figure 5.4(a) or the 6×6 'chess' board in figure 5.4(b) can be used.

Figure 5.4(a)

5.4(b)

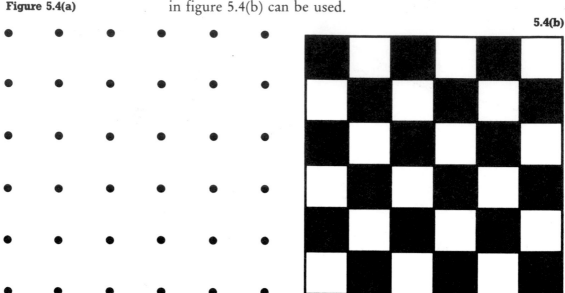

Playing alternately, each of two players places a symbol (say an 'X' for player 1 and a '0' for player 2) at a point on the grid, or a coloured counter in a square if the board is used. Each player tries to avoid placing four 'Xs' or '0s' at the corners of a square and a player wins when the opponent is forced to make a square or inadvertently does so. Squares do not have to be made up of horizontal/vertical lines, figure 5.5 shows some ways in which they can be formed.

Much careful attention is needed to avoid making 'unexpected' squares. Those familiar with the 'How many squares on a chessboard?' problem may start to think in a new light after playing 'Hip' (see suggested investigation (ii)). (For readers unfamiliar with the problem, an 8×8 chessboard has many more than 64 'squares' if all possible squares made up from lines parallel to the sides of the board are counted, the total number of squares is in excess of 200.)

Investigations

(i) Try simplified games on 2×2, 3×3, 4×4, 5×5 boards. What happens in each case?

40

(ii) For each board from 2×2 to 6×6, how many possible squares can be formed on the grid? Is there a pattern? Can the results be generalised to a n×n grid?

(iii) Can either player develop a winning strategy?

(iv) Consider the extension of the game to larger boards. Also try rectangular boards.

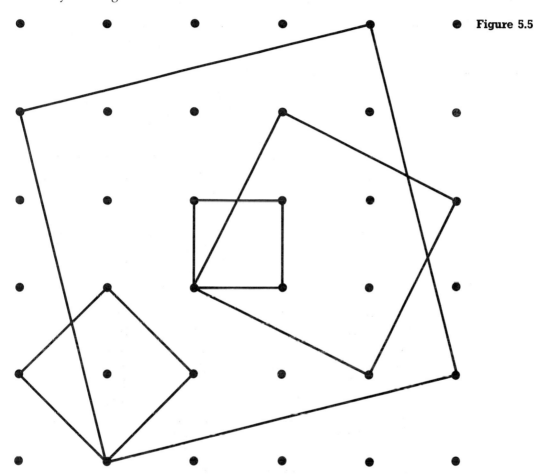

Figure 5.5

5.4 Boxes and Variations

The traditional game of *Boxes* is simple. A rectangular grid of dots (for example figure 5.6) is drawn. Two players take turns to join any two neighbouring dots with a line (diagonals are not allowed). If a player can complete a small square (box) on a turn then that box is 'won' and the player puts his/her initial

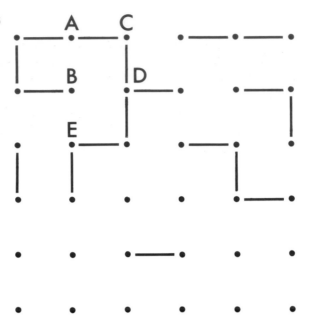

Figure 5.6

inside it and has another turn. In figure 5.6 the player to move could join AB to win a box, then BD to win a second and BE to win a third.

The Worm

This is played in the same way as *Boxes*. Two players play alternately but, on each move, the player must continue from one of the ends of the existing pattern (the 'worm') the 'worm' may not cross itself. A player loses if forced to join the worm back on to itself, figure 5.7 shows a position in which the player to move next must lose.

Figure 5.7

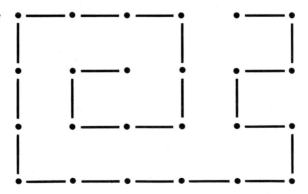

Empire

This version is played in the same way as *Boxes* but each completed box will contain a number (see for example figure 5.8). The winner is the player with the highest total contained within captured boxes.

Clearly there are many possible types of numbers which may be placed in the boxes and games with fractions, decimals, powers, square roots etc. could easily be devised.

Figure 5.8

+1	-5	+2	-3	+4
+6	-4	+7	-2	+1
-6	+4	-7	+3	+5
+6	-1	+4	-3	+2
-1	-2	+3	-6	+5

Investigations

(i)   Consider *Boxes* played on rectangular grids with 4, 6, 8, 10 ... dots. Which player should win in each case?

(ii) What is the largest *worm* possible on an 8×8 grid? Can you generalise to a grid of any size?

(iii) On a 6×6 grid what is the maximum angle through which the worm can turn during a game?

(iv) If *Empire* is played on a grid with 12 squares, suggest the fairest way of distributing the numbers $-6, -5, ..., -1, +1, ..., +6$ on the grid.

(v)   Invent and investigate a game of *fighting worms* in which two players each have a separate worm and you lose if either (a) the opponent's worm bites yours or (b) you are forced to bite yourself!

5.5 Sprouts

The origins of a game may often be difficult to unravel, and even the inventor may not be completely clear how the game evolved; however the background to this game is known in detail. It was invented in Cambridge on the afternoon of Tuesday, 21 February 1967 by John Conway and one of his research students, Michael Paterson. The game has since been widely played, it leads to some interesting diagrams and produces a feel for basic topology. Conway called the game *Sprouts*; it quickly became very popular in Cambridge and elsewhere and the alternative name of *Measles* was suggested because 'it's catching and breaks out in spots'!

An agreed number of dots (say three) is placed on a piece of paper. Two players take turns to play. At a turn a player joins two existing dots (the line can be curved or straight) *and* places a new dot somewhere on the line drawn.

Figure 5.9

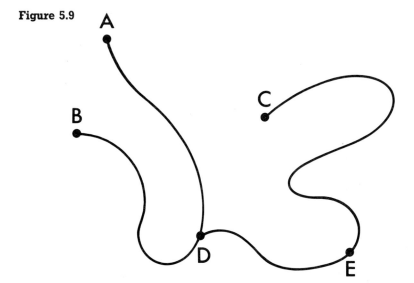

For example, in figure 5.9, if A,B,C were the original points, the first player might play be joining A to B and placing a new dot at D. The second player might now join D to C, introducing a new dot at E and so on. A line may not cross itself or another line and no dot may have more than three lines going from it (thus in figure 5.9, the point D cannot be used again, a line cannot travel *through* an existing dot). The first player who cannot make a legal move loses. Since there are no restrictions on the shape of the line joining two points some intricate patterns emerge!

Investigations

(i)   Consider a game with only two dots, who wins?
What about three dots?

(ii)   Can you find a pattern involving the number of moves
possible for a given number of starting dots?

(iii) Is there a winning strategy?

5.6 Brussels Sprouts

This is a delightful variation of *Sprouts*. Instead of 'blobs',
crosses are used (see figure 5.10).

Each move must join the arms of two existing crosses and
generate a new cross (although two of the arms of the new
cross will already have been used). Thus, in figure 5.10, if the
game starts with crosses at A,B,C,D, the first move might be
the line shown joining A to D with a new cross appearing at E.
As in *Sprouts* players play alternately and lines must not cross
other lines or go through other crosses. The first player who
cannot make a move is the loser.

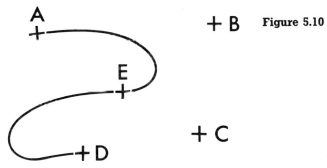

Figure 5.10

Although, at first sight, the game appears to involve
decisions and skill, the result is predetermined once the initial
number of crosses and the identity of the starting player have
been agreed! The investigations which follow will show why
this is so.

Investigations

(i)   Play games starting with three crosses. For how many
moves does each game last?
How often does the first player win?
How often does the second player win?

(ii) Play games starting with different numbers of crosses. For each version keep a record of the number of moves and the winning player. Can you find a pattern?

(iii) Which player should win for a given number of crosses?

(iv) Investigate a game with five-pointed stars instead of crosses.

6 GEOMETRICAL GAMES WITH BOARDS

Board games can range from the elaborate, commercially-packaged variety to those which can be played with equipment which is easily available and can be assembled in a few minutes. The presence of a board and playing pieces of some kind will usually make a game visually more attractive and hence of immediate appeal to potential players. In a school classroom a teacher has to balance this increased attractiveness against the problems which the provision and distribution of equipment might entail, although for many games such equipment is very simple. This chapter contains games of varying complexity: some are available commercially but all could easily be 'manufactured' using basic materials like cardboard, counters, buttons etc.

6.1 Next

This game was invented by Claude Soucie who also invented *Divide and Conquer* (chapter 3). According to a letter received from Mrs Soucie, Claude was born in Quebec and grew up in the Great Depression, money was a problem and toys and games a luxury so he decided to invent games of his own. *Next* can be played by people of *any* age (we have experience of a three year old playing the game)!

A board divided into nine regions is drawn (see figure 6.1). Nine counters are needed, 3 red, 3 blue and 3 yellow. Two players play alternately and, at a turn, place a counter in a vacant space on the board, no two counters of the same colour may be placed in regions with a common boundary. The first player unable to make a legal move is the loser. (It is suggested that a game might consist of nine rounds: in round 1, the first counter must be placed in region '1', in round 2 the first counter must be placed in region '2' and so on.)

Links with simple topological problems, especially the 'Four Colour Map Problem', which states that any map needs a maximum of four colours if no two neighbouring regions are to have the same colour (see for example Courant and Robbins (1969)) will be apparent. As an interesting variant a *real* map could be used for example counties of England, states of the USA or countries of Europe, thus giving a useful cross-curricular link.

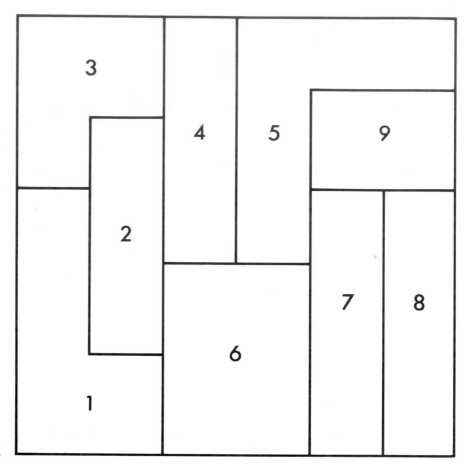

Figure 6.1

Investigations

(i)   In how many ways can the first two counters be placed
      (a) if they are all different colours and (b) if they are all the
      same colour?
      How many ways are there for the first three counters?

(ii) What is the smallest number of counters which can be put
      on the board before it is impossible to place any more?
      Draw a diagram to show the position.

(iii) Experiment with different size boards (design your own)
      and different numbers of counters.

6.2 Traffic Lights

This is a simple but thought provoking game based on *Noughts
and Crosses* and invented by Alan Parr.

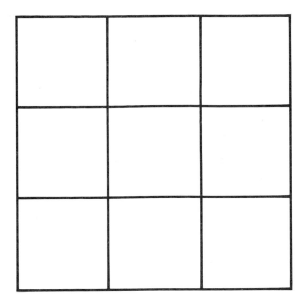

Figure 6.2

Children playing 'Traffic Lights'

The game is played on a 3×3 board (figure 6.2) using a stock of red, orange and green counters (nine of each colour is the maximum number required). Two players play alternately and, at a turn, can:

  (a) put a red counter in an empty square,

or (b) replace a red counter with an orange one,

or (c) replace an orange counter with a green one.

The winner is the first player to complete a line of three counters of the same colour (vertically, horizontally or diagonally, as in *Noughts and Crosses*).

Possible variations include (a) making a simpler game by using only two colours, (b) playing on a 4×4 grid and (c) allowing a fourth option on a player's turn, namely removing a green counter from the board.

The game was exhaustively analysed by computer in America with the conclusion that the first player should win although the analysis did not show how! The actual game is simple but its analysis can be complex.

Investigations

(i) How many positions are possible after each player has made one move?

(ii) What is the maximum number of pieces of one colour which can be on the board without a line being made?

(iii) How many moves are there in the shortest possible game? How many moves are there in the longest possible game?

(iv) Is a draw possible?

(v) Investigate the above questions for a 4×4 board.

6.3 Quadromania

This game was invented by Graham Ellsbury, a landscape architect. It is produced commercially by Red Dragon Games Limited. Essentially it is extremely simple and could be played by children of primary school age. The skills needed involve little more than classification of shapes and the ability to operate a simple scoring system.

The board (figure 6.3) consists of a 4×4 grid of dots and 16 playing pieces as shown on figure 6.4 are needed.

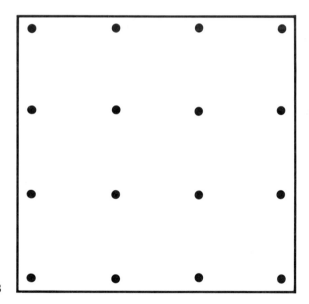

Figure 6.3

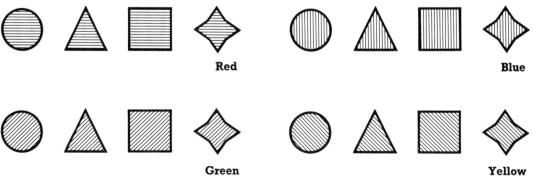

Figure 6.4

Two players make alternate moves. One player is the 'colour' player and the other the 'shape' player. The colour player starts and places any piece on any point: the shape player now follows and places another piece. Once a point is occupied the piece on it cannot be moved and play continues until all pieces have been placed. The object of the game is to score points by forming 'quads' and 'rows': a 'quad' is a 2×2 formation of pieces and a 'row' is a vertical, horizontal or diagonal line of pieces (see figure 6.5).

(A piece can be in any number of 'quads' or 'rows' and often a player will find that a move results in points being scored for *both* players.)

Scoring is as follows:

The *colour* player scores:

   2 points for each 'quad' of four different colours

   3 points for each 'row' of four different colours

   5 points for each 'row' of four identical colours

  10 points for each 'quad' of four identical colours

The *shape* player scores in the same way but with shapes instead of colours.

The winner is the first player to score an agreed number of points or win an agreed number of games.

Although the equipment is fun to make, the game could be played with cards from an ordinary pack of playing cards using the A,K,Q,J from each suit.

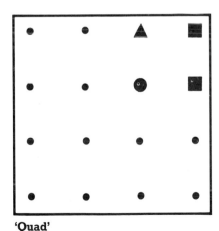

'Quad'

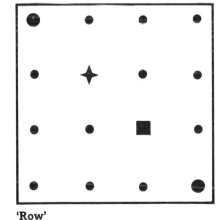

'Row'

Figure 6.5

Investigations

(i)   What are the highest and lowest individual scores possible? Are all scores between these possible?

(ii) Is it possible to have a game where both players score zero?

(iii) How many 'quads' are there on a 4×4 board?
How many 'rows'?

(iv) Is a tie possible?

(v) Investigate other scoring systems.

6.4 Black

Black is a game invented by William Black which has close links with the games of *September* (Paradigm Games) and *Continuo* (Hiron Games) which have been marketed in recent years. A squared board with one corner square shaded is needed (for example see figure 6.6):

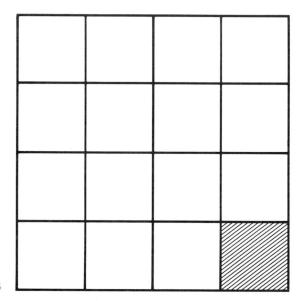

Figure 6.6

A supply of shapes as shown in figure 6.7 is needed (about 10 of each will normally be sufficient). Two players alternate and, at a turn, can play any of the shapes.

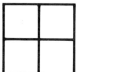

Figure 6.7

The first player must begin with the cross in the top left hand corner, the second player must then join the path from the previous piece for example

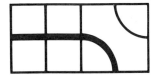

Figure 6.8

but must not go to the edge of the board. The next two moves might lead to:

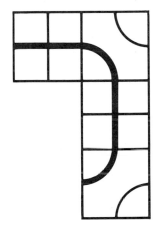

Figure 6.9

A continuous path must be maintained and a player wins if he/she reaches the shaded square but loses if he/she is forced to join the path to the edge of the board.

Investigations

(i)   On a 3×3 board how many games are possible?
      How many give the first player a win, how many the second?

(ii) If all 15 unshaded squares on a 4×4 board are used, how many games are possible?
      In how many of these does a player win by reaching the shaded square?

(iii) Investigate games with different shapes to place on the board (for example a square with diagonals as a playing piece).

6.5 September

This game was invented by Danny Kishon, an 'ex-student of Biochemistry, part-time magician and tour guide', and first produced by Paradigm Games in 1986.

In its simplest form it is played on the board shown in figure 6.10.

Figure 6.10

Each of the two players has a set of seven 'straight' pieces which are one unit long and three 'L' pieces (see figure 6.11), one player's pieces are red, the other yellow.

Players place a piece on the board alternately, red connecting the circles and yellow the triangles. The aim is to make a continuous line across the board, red vertically, yellow horizontally. If, after all the pieces have been played, neither player has succeeded in making a line then, in phase two, players can pick up any one of their pieces and place it elsewhere.

(A harder version of *September* uses a 10×10 board and extra playing pieces of different shapes.)

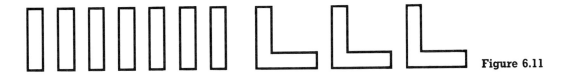

Figure 6.11

Investigations

(i) How many different paths across the board are possible and what are their lengths?
What is the longest possible path?

(ii) Is a draw (by stalemate) possible?

(iii) Invent a three-dimensional form of the game for three players.

6.6 Continuo

Continuo was invented by Maureen Hiron (Hiron Games) on April 1 1982: 'It just flashed into my head as I was watching TV and listening to Bach on the radio in the background... I grabbed an empty Kelloggs packet, scissors, ruler, coloured markers, and two hours later had made the first set of *Continuo*'. The game was voted 'Game of the year' in 1982.

Continuo is played with 42 square cards with coloured squares on them like those shown in figure 6.12.

The aim is to make 'chains' of single colours with adjoining cards (for example yellow and blue chains are shown in figure 6.12).

Players draw in turn from the 'pack' of cards which is placed face down, one card is turned up and placed on the table to start the game. Thereafter points are scored for lengths

Figure 6.12

The game of 'Continuo'

of chains completed, in the figure 8 points would be scored, 4 each for the blue and yellow chains. The cards are of three types (see figure 6.13).

There is also a triangular version of the game *Triangulo Continuo*.

1	2	3	1
2	2	3	3
3	3	2	2
1	3	2	1

A: 12 of these (3 colours)

1	3	1	2
3	3	1	1
1	1	3	3
2	1	3	1

B: 24 of these (3 colours)

1	2	1	2
2	2	1	1
1	1	2	2
2	1	2	1

C: 6 of these (2 colours)

Figure 6.13

Investigations

(i)   Make a full set of 42 cards and investigate symmetries on the cards.

(ii) Design and make the cards for equivalent 2×2 and 3×3 versions of the game. How many cards will there be?

(iii) What is the maximum possible score with all the cards in each game? (i.e. 2×2, 3×3 and 4×4).

6.7 Entropy

Eric Solomon, a computer scientist and also a former British croquet champion, has invented a number of games: *Entropy* is one of them (another is *Black Box*, see chapter 7). The game is one which has an appealing simplicity and elegance. It has been marketed under the name *Vice Versa* but the name *Entropy* reflects the law of thermodynamics which recognises that all processes result in an increasing amount of disorder in the world at large. The game is played on a 5×5 board (figure 6.14).

25 counters are needed: 5 of each of the colours red, blue, white, green and yellow. One player is designated as the 'Experimenter' (E) and is attempting to build an ordered situation, the other is the 'Universe' (U) attempting to hinder the 'Experimenter'. Play consists of six rounds. In each round 'U' nominates 4 counters (5 in the first round) and 'E' positions them anywhere in vacant positions on the board. 'U' is then allowed to slide any two counters horizontally or vertically (no jumping is allowed) into new positions. In the last round, since all squares are now occupied, 'U' has no slides to make.

57

When all the counters have been placed 'E' receives a score based on the amount of symmetry he/she has been able to force into the final pattern. In every row/column each group of two adjacent counters in a symmetrical pattern scores 2 points; patterns of 3,4,5 counters score 3,4,5 points. One counter may contribute to several scoring patterns. The examples below will clarify the scoring.

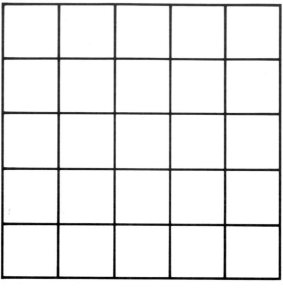

Figure 6.14

RWRBB   the *RWR* scores 3 and the *BB* scores 2 which gives a total of 5.

RGGGB   *GG* scores 2 in positions 2 and 3 and a further 2 in positions 3 and 4. The whole *GGG* scores 3. The total is 7.

WGWBW   *WGW* scores 3, *WBW* scores 3 which gives a total of 6.

GWBGR   this does not have any symmetrical groups so the total is 0.

YYBYY   the two *YY* pairs score 2 each, the central *YBY* scores 3, the whole group scores 5. The total is 12.

A complete row of one colour would score 30, 8 for four pairs, 9 for three threes, 8 for two fours and 5 for the five.

The following is an example of a complete layout:

R	Y	Y	Y	B	7
G	B	R	R	B	6
W	G	Y	B	W	0
W	R	G	G	W	2
W	R	Y	G	B	0
7	2	6	2	8	Total 40

On completion of a 'round' the roles of 'E' and 'U' are reversed and the new 'E' player attempts to beat the previous 'Es' score.

Investigations

(i) What is the maximum score that could be made?

(ii) Is it possible to score zero? If not what is the minimum score?

(iii) Is it possible to make every score between the maximum and minimum scores?

(iv) On a 2×2 board with two red and two blue counters, what scores are possible?

(v) Investigate the possibilities on a 3×3 board with three colours. Also consider other variations.

6.8 Intersection

From a mathematical point of view this game provides a fruitful area for number work, especially number patterns, in a *geometric* setting.

The game, for two players, uses a 5×5 board and five sets of counters of different colours: 3 red, 4 blue, 5 green, 6 yellow and 7 black. At the start of the game the counters are distributed randomly on the board. The first player (we will designate him/her as the 'row' player) puts a marker against one of the rows and then the second player (the 'column' player) puts a marker against one of the columns and removes the counter indicated by the *intersection* of the two markers (see for example figure 6.15 in which the shaded piece would be removed).

The 'row' player now moves his/her marker to a new row and removes the counter at the new intersection. Play continues with alternate moves until a player is unable to take a counter. Scoring at the end of the game is as follows:
If a player has 7 counters of one colour.....28 points
6 counters of one colour.....21 points
5 counters of one colour.....15 points
4 counters of one colour.....10 points
3 counters of one colour..... 6 points
2 counters of one colour..... 3 points
1 counter of a colour........... 1 point

If a player possesses counters of a colour which is not held by the opponent then the score for that colour is doubled (for example if one player has 4 blacks and the other 3 are still on the board, the score is $2 \times 10 = 20$ points). The player with the higher points total is the winner.

A *simplified* game could be played without the board with each player simply having a free choice of counters at each turn.

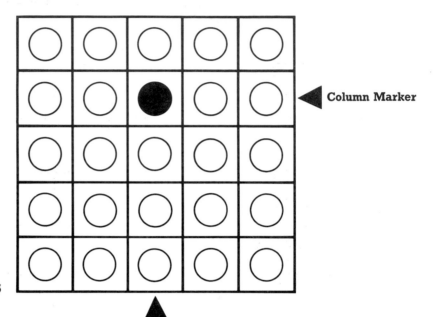

Figure 6.15

Column Marker

Row Marker

Investigations

(i) What is the smallest number of moves possible before a game ends?
What is the largest number?

(ii) What is the highest score possible for an individual player? Make a list of all possible scores.

(iii) Consider and investigate a game on (i) a 3×3 board, (ii) a 4×4 board. In each case experiment with different combinations of coloured counters.

6.9 Face Ache

This game is described in Tapson, (1986). It is played by two players on a grid of squares of *any* shape or size (figure 6.16 gives some examples). A *face* is drawn on one of the squares.

Each player in turn shades in a complete rectangle of any size. The player who is forced to shade in the face loses the game. (N.B. It may be necessary to make clear to pupils that any square is also a rectangle!)

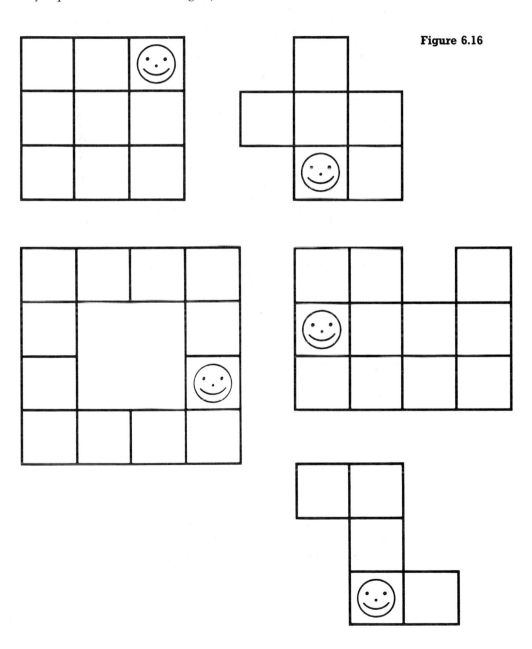

Figure 6.16

Investigations

(i) On a 2×2 board how many possible moves are open to the first player?

(ii) Investigate 3×3, 4×4 and 5×5 boards. How many *distinct* positions are there for the face?

(iii) How many distinct positions for the face are there on different rectangular boards, for example 2×3, 3×5 . . .?

(iv) Invent a 3-dimensional version with a 3×3×3 cube. ('Multilink' blocks may be useful!)

6.10 Chomp

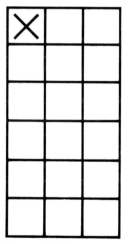

Figure 6.18

Chomp was invented by David Gale, a mathematician and economist at the University of California. A set of counters is placed on a rectangular grid, the counter in the bottom left hand corner is of a different colour from the rest. Two players take turns to remove counters as follows: any counter is selected and all the counters which are in the rectangle in which this counter occupies the bottom left hand corner are removed. The object of the game is to force your opponent to take the 'poison' counter in the bottom left hand corner. Figure 6.17 shows an example of a game.

In the illustrated game the first player loses after seven moves in all.

The following related problem is to be found in Robin, (1989):

A bar of chocolate has 3×6 squares with one corner poisoned. Each player in turns breaks the chocolate (in a straight line along the grooves) and eats the piece he breaks off. The player to leave his opponent with the single poisoned piece is the winner.

Investigations

(i) How many games are possible on a 3×3 grid?
How many are possible on a 4×4 grid?

(ii) What are (a) the shortest and (b) the longest games possible on 3×3, 4×4 and 5×5 grids?

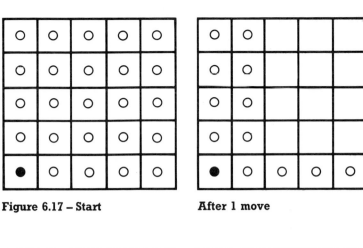

Figure 6.17 – Start

After 1 move

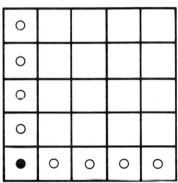

After 2 moves

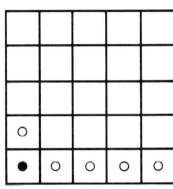

After 3 moves

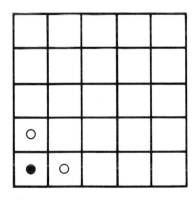

After 4 moves

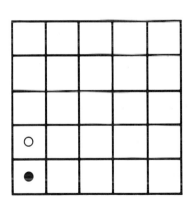

After 5 moves

(iii) Investigate similar problems for non-square grids for example 2×3, 3×5, . . .

(iv) On a square grid, what is the 'best' opening move and why?

7 INFERENTIAL GAMES

The games in this chapter are different from those elsewhere in the book. In most of the games previously described, two players have the same goal and (more or less) equal chances, the only real point of difference is that the first player may, or may not, have an advantage. In the games in this section the roles are usually unequal: one player sets a problem which the other has to decipher. Thus there can be considerable flexibility in using these games. The teacher can be the question master and the class can be his/her collective opponent, or the class might work in groups, each group with its own question master. The teacher can offer problems which can be solved for homework and another possibility may involve versions where pupils can work against a computer.

Although the games generally need more detailed description than those in other chapters (and look superficially more complex) they do repay close scrutiny and they can be adapted to levels which are suitable for young children. For most of the games, the effort and time invested in careful study will be amply repaid by the discovery of some fascinating ideas and some useful material for a classroom.

Perhaps the best known game which comes into the category of this chapter is *Mastermind*. It is so well known that the full details are not included here. The game is produced by Invicta Plastics who first marketed it in the early 1970s but earlier versions under names like *Bulls and Cows* and *Dots and Stars* had been around much earlier.

In *Dots and Stars* one player chooses a number of (say) four digits: the other guesses and receives a *dot* for each correct digit and a *star* for each correct digit in its correct place: thus if the number chosen is 1234 and the guess is 1354 then one dot (for the '3') and two stars for the '1' and '4' would be awarded. The second player tries to discover the number in as few guesses as possible. Alternatively *both* players invent a number and guess alternately with the winner being the first player to deduce the opponent's number. The familiar *Mastermind* box (see illustration) shows a picture of a gentleman seated and a chinese girl standing and has been duplicated on 55 million games and variations and sold in 80 countries with rules in 33 languages. The famous photograph appeared after Mr Bill Woodward, an owner of women's hairdressing shops, was asked to sit for a picture to use on the front cover with a white cat on his lap. According to Invicta, 'This cat peed on Bill's lap so we asked a beautiful chinese girl to stand alongside Bill!' *Mastermind* in its many versions became a cult with an extensive following and in its heyday attracted many competitions and puzzle books, see for example Ault (1976) or Ault (1978).

The game of 'Mastermind'

7.1 Lap

At first sight this might appear to be a fairly uninspiring game and it is not until you actually try it that you begin to appreciate its full subtlety. But, like many games descended from it, it is a lovely game. It comes from Sackson (1969), see the notes under *Suggested further reading* at the end of the book.

Lap is by Lech Pijanowski, a Polish film critic. The name is simply Lech's initials. Two players each need a pencil and a sheet of squared paper on which they outline two 8×8 squres each containing 64 cells. The cells are defined by a number and a letter (see figure 7.1).

Both players, keeping their paper out of sight of each other, divide one of the 8×8 squares into four continuous sections which are labelled W,X,Y,Z. The sectors must each contain 16 cells (see for example figure 7.2).

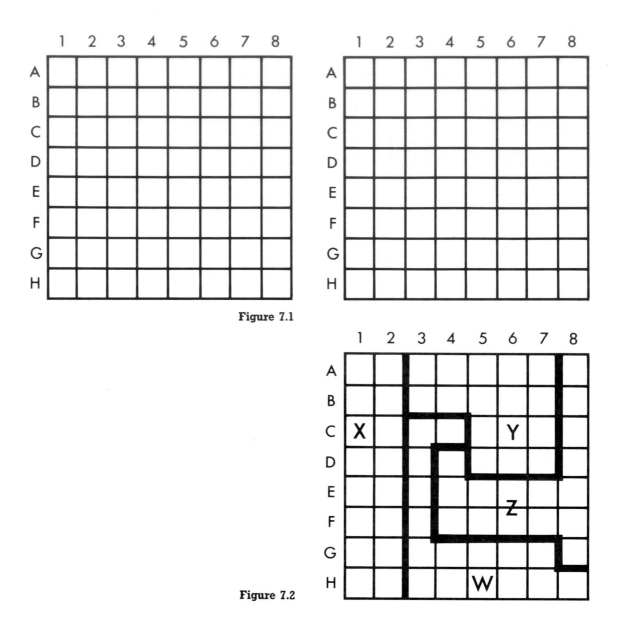

Figure 7.1

Figure 7.2

The second 8×8 square is used to reconstruct the opponent's sectors as information about them is obtained.

In turn each player calls the coordinates of 4 cells forming a 2×2 square for example F-G-3-4 would represent cells F3, F4, G3, G4. The opponent responds by giving the sectors contained in these cells: thus the answer to F-G-3-4 in figure 7.2 would be 'three in W and one in Z'. As soon as a player thinks he/she has reconstructed the opponent's sectors, the game is over except that, if the opponent played second he/she can have one more turn.

A reconstructed pattern must be exactly the same as the original to be correct. If only one player submits a pattern, he/she wins or loses depending on whether the pattern is correct or not. If both players submit at the same time, the one with the greater number of cells correct is the winner.

The following are further examples of calls and replies based on figure 7.2:

Call: A-B-7-8   Reply: 2 in Y, 2 in Z.
Call: C-D-1-2   Reply: 4 in X.
Call: C-D-4-5   Reply: 1 in W, 2 in Y, 1 in Z.

Investigations

(i) Play the game with a 4×4 grid, each region now to contain 4 cells. Find as many divisions as possible which leave (a) four congruent regions, (b) a figure with line or rotational symmetry.

(ii) Now try the questions in (i) for a 6×6 board.

(iii) What are the easiest/hardest patterns to identify?

(iv) Assuming that the grid is to be divided into four regions of equal area, what size grids can you play on?
Can you play on any even sided grid?
How could you organise play on an odd sided grid? (for example on a 5×5 grid you could exclude the central square from the playing area)
What can you discover about squares of odd numbers?

7.2 Zone X

This was produced by Invicta as a follow up to the better known *Mastermind* (see page 64). It is similar to *Lap* though probably much less exciting to play and it has a strong resemblance to the popular game of *Battleships*. *Zone X* offers an excellent opportunity to develop work on coordinates.

Play is on a 15×15 grid. One player (unseen by the other) draws two lines which intersect at a point on the grid (for example G8 in figure 7.3) and then labels the four regions created 'red', 'green', 'yellow' and 'blue'. The other player has a pegboard with 15×15 holes and a supply of red, green, yellow and blue pegs, together with a few white ones. He/she calls out the coordinates of a point and is told the colour of the zone in which the point lies or, exceptionally, that it lies on a

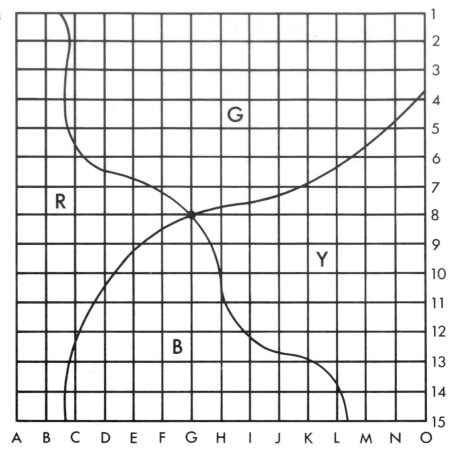

Figure 7.3

line, in which case it can be denoted by a white peg. The aim is to deduce the coordinates of the point of intersection of the lines in as few guesses as possible.

The following are examples of responses using figure 7.3: D9 gets the response 'red', K6 gets the response 'green', K7 gets the response 'white' and so on.

Investigations

(i) Suppose the game is played with *straight* lines. What is the minimum number of questions needed to identify one of the lines?
What properties can you find for points on vertical, horizontal and other lines?

(ii) What form might the game take if three lines were used?
How many regions will there be if the lines meet at a single point?
If they do not, how many regions will there be?
What about the same questions for 4, 5, 6 ... lines?

7.3 Rhino and Elephant

(Two computer games from the *Microsmile* collection.)

These games are variations of *Zone X*. The computer selects one point on a grid and the player has to locate it in as few moves as possible. In *Elephant* each time the player suggests a pair of coordinates the computer gives the *distance* between the target point and the chosen point whilst in *Rhino* the computer gives the *distance moving along the vertical/horizontal lines of the grid*.

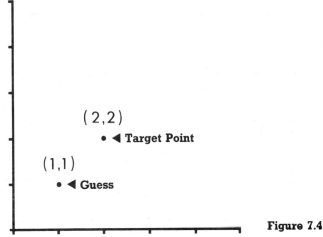

Figure 7.4

In figure 7.4 the computer would give the answer 1.4 (i.e. the square root of 2) in *Elephant* and the answer 2 in *Rhino*.

The game can, of course, be played *without* a computer in a variety of classroom settings and *Rhino* in particular is ideal for young children. The whole field of coordinate work is opened up as well as work on Pythagoras, square roots, loci, rational/irrational numbers etc.

As in *Zone X*, the aim is to locate the target point in as few guesses as possible.

Investigations

(Consider the games *Elephant* and *Rhino* separately.)

(i) How many points on the grid are still possible candidates after the first question has been asked?

(ii) What is the smallest number of questions you need to ask to be certain of identifying the chosen point?

(iii) What is the best point to choose for your first guess? How should you decide on your second guess?

(iv) Try the above questions with different sizes of board.

$\underline{7.4}$ White Box

Readers may be familiar with the game of *Black Box* (Waddington) which was invented by Eric Solomon (see chapter 6 for information about Eric who also invented the game of *Entropy* described there).

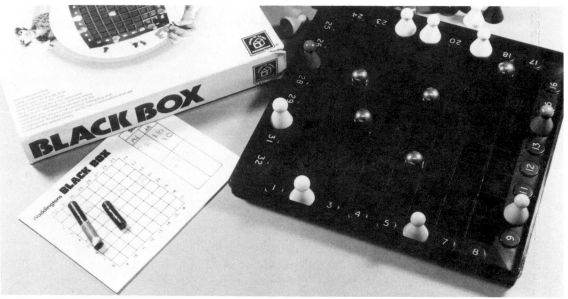

The game of 'Black Box'

Black Box followed the *Mastermind* craze in the early/middle 1970s. In the game one player takes the role of an experimenter attempting to deduce the chemical structure of an unknown material by observing the effect the substance has upon rays which are fired at it. Whilst the actual science is rather fanciful the game does offer some good insights into scientific method. It is an excellent game and has been included in the MEP primary computer package *Investigations and problem solving in the primary school*. The game of *White Box* was invented by Alan Parr using a grid of triangles (rather than squares as in *Black Box*) and it thus avoids some of the complexities and ambiguities of *Black Box*, therefore making it a more accessible game for the beginner.

White Box is played on a hexagonal grid made up of triangular cells labelled as in figure 7.5.

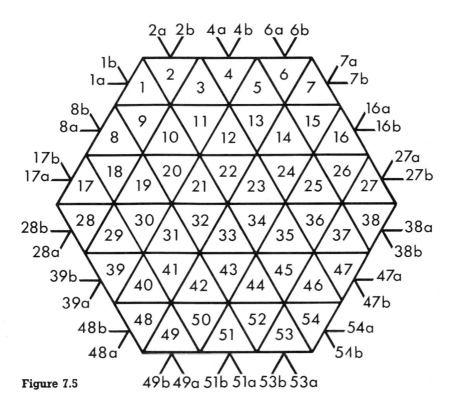

Figure 7.5

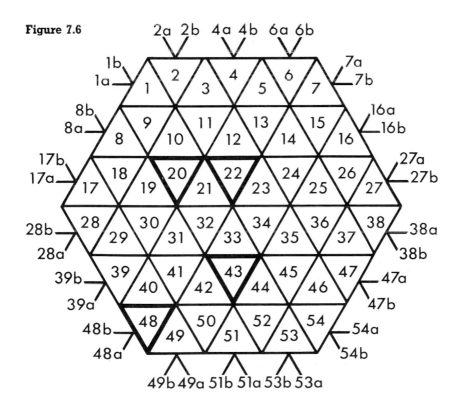

Figure 7.6

Two players each have a hexagon which they keep to themselves. One player sketches in an agreed number of triangles (say 4) and the sides of these now act as mirrors. The task of the second player is to discover the whereabouts of these mirrors by injecting rays of light and being told by the first player where a ray will emerge. The aim is to ascertain the position of the mirrors in as few guesses as possible.

As examples of questions/answers during a game, consider figure 7.6.

A ray injected at 49b would be reflected by the mirror at 43 and emerge at 39b. A ray entering at 7a would hit the mirror at 43, be reflected up to the mirror at 20, across to the mirror at 22, down to the mirror at 48 and emerge at 17b (so if the player injects a ray at 7a, he/she is told that it emerges at 17b).

The game has enormous potential not just for its inferential value but also in encouraging work on coordinates, reflections etc and cross-curricular links with science since the game will certainly reinforce the fact that 'angle of incidence = angle of reflection'.

Investigations

(i)   Suppose there is one mirror only. What is the smallest number of rays which will guarantee that you can identify this mirror?

(ii) Consider question (i) with 2, 3, 4 . . . mirrors.

(iii) Can a ray get lost and never emerge?

(iv) If a ray entering at P emerges at Q, does a ray entering at Q emerge at P?

(v)   What is the maximum number of reflections a ray can undergo?

(vi) Investigate any patterns you can find relating the reference numbers of the ingoing and outgoing rays.

7.5 Latino

This has been described as 'a gem of a game'. It is very much in the *Lap* and *Mastermind* family in that you retrieve information in a form which is not immediately useable and must be interpreted before you can decode what it has to offer. The game was invented in the USA by Steve Wilson and, for classroom use, it has even more potential than *Lap* or *Mastermind* in that its basis is strongly mathematical.

Two players each make up an 8×8 Latin Square (i.e. an array in which each column and each row contains exactly one of the numbers 1, 2, 3, 4, 5, 6, 7, 8, see figure 7.7)

Figure 7.7

7	2	8	1	5	6	3	4	8
1	7	2	8	6	3	4	5	7
4	8	1	2	7	5	6	3	6
6	1	3	7	8	4	5	2	5
5	6	7	4	3	1	2	8	4
3	4	5	6	2	7	8	1	3
2	3	4	5	1	8	7	6	2
8	5	6	3	4	2	1	7	1

A   B   C   D   E   F   G   H

In turn players question their opponent about his/her square. You can ask for the sum of any 2/3 consecutive numbers in a row or column, for example in figure 7.7:

if you ask 'D345', the answer is '17'
if you ask 'DE4', the answer is '7'.

When one player thinks that he/she knows the opponent's square, the game ends. Both players now produce copies of what they think the squares look like and the one who has most numbers correct is the winner.

Any size board can be used and it is probably best to begin on a 4×4 or 6×6 board. (For a full discussion of Latin Squares of different sizes, the reader might like to consult Ball and Coxeter (1974).)

Investigations

(i) Can you construct a Latin Square of any order? Try from 1×1 up to 10×10.

(ii) Look at the totals in each row and column for different size squares. How do they change for different sizes?

(iii) On a 6×6 board the following is a set of questions and answers. Can you deduce the numbers on the board?
ABC1 = 13 DE1 = 6 F123 = 11 F45 = 6 DEF6 = 12
BC6 = 7 B456 = 10 CDE5 = 9 D234 = 9 E234 = 12
ABC3 = 11 BC5 = 3 C23 = 8

(iv) When you enquire about pairs of numbers, what totals are possible?
What about trios?

(v) For a given arrangement, what is the minimum number of enquiries which would allow a complete solution?

7.6 Eleusis (pronounced El – lew – sis)

This game first appeared about thirty years ago and was the first and most famous of a family of 'inductive' card games. Its particular point of interest is that it runs counter to conventional card games in which players attempt to play as correctly as possible within the known rules of the game. In *Eleusis* there is only one rule but the players do not know what it is! The game is fully described in Abbott (1963) and Abbott (1977). It was publicised by Martin Gardner (for example Gardner (1971)) and people were attracted particularly by its pseudo-religious overtones in which the rule setter came to be thought of as God and the players as seekers after divine truth. In fact Abbott became dissatisfied with the basic game and developed it into a revised version called *New Eleusis* which expanded these aspects still further by allowing for Prophets and even False Prophets to appear!

At least three players, and an ordinary pack of 52 cards are needed. The dealer makes up a secret rule (see below for examples) which is not revealed to any of the players. Each player then seeks to determine the rule by playing cards and observing which obey the rule and which do not.

The dealer deals the entire pack between the other players

except for the last card which is placed face up in the centre of the table (to achieve equal hands for each player, it may be necessary to remove one or more cards at the start). The first player places a card on the starter card and the dealer announces 'right' or 'wrong' depending on whether or not the card conforms to the secret rule, if 'right' the player leaves the card in the centre, if 'wrong' the card is left face up in front of the player. The next player now plays in the same way and so on, the table will look something like figure 7.8 after a number of turns.

Figure 7.8

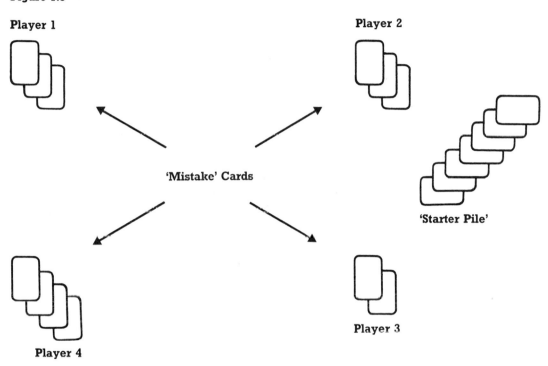

Play continues until all cards have been played. The scoring system in the 'real' game is complex, see Abbott (1963), but, for a simple game it is suggested that the player with the smallest number of 'mistake' cards is the winner.

The following are examples of possible secret rules (assume that ace=1, jack=11, queen=12, king=13):

(a) if the last card is red, play a black; if black, play a red;
(b) if the last card is odd, play an even; if even, play an odd;
(c) if the last card is in the range ace to 7, play a card from the range 8 to king and vice-versa;
(d) make the sum of the last card and the card played a perfect square (or a prime number, or a multiple of 3 etc.).

Investigations

(i) Invent some secret rules.

(ii) If the rule is 'make the sum of the last card and the card played a perfect square', how many possible 'right' plays are possible if the last card is a '7'?
How about other numbers from 1 to 13?
Is there any pattern?

(iii) Investigate the problem in (ii) if the rule is 'make the product of the last card and the card played a multiple of 3 or 5'.

(iv) Invent a simplified game with a pack of cards numbered 1 to 20.

8 USING GAMES WITH CHILDREN

In this chapter we offer some comments and reflections on the use of games in the classroom. Nearly all children enjoy playing games and what we would wish to do is to capitalise upon this enjoyment within the framework of mathematics. The aim of this book is to help the teacher build a good environment for the learning of mathematics and to make use of children's enthusiasm as a powerful motivating factor. It is crucial that games do not become just another topic in a mathematics curriculum, rather they should be seen as a useful aid which can be used when appropriate to foster cooperative and child-centred learning.

The majority of the games in chapters 2 to 7 have been tried out with pupils whose ages ranged from 7 to 18. Varying degrees of success were obtained and sometimes a game (with associated investigations) which worked well with one group proved a complete flop with another. Often the same game would be described by one pupil as 'boring' and by another as 'exciting'. We give here a few examples of (a) introductory sheets which have been used with pupils, (b) pieces of pupils' work and (c) pupil reactions. Tucked away in these 'snapshots' of games in action in the classroom we hope the reader will find both ideas to use and food for thought.

A number of common themes in the work which has been done may well be worth highlighting:

- Pupils were always allowed to *play* a game first: sometimes this involved the making of simple equipment before starting.
- The *investigation* phase was one in which pupils were asked to invent ways of recording games and to think of variations. Faced with a difficult problem/game/investigation, pupils were always encouraged to invent simpler situations for themselves (thus for example if a game requires a 4×4 grid, it is often worth considering the same game on a 2×2 or 3×3 grid first). Compare this approach with the philosophy of George Polya: 'If you cannot solve the proposed problem, try to solve first some related problem' (Polya (1957)).
- Pupils were always asked to produce a *write-up* which included a description of the game in their own words, some discussion of what they had investigated and their comments on the game itself.

The following pages contain examples of worksheets and pupils' work.

Westbury

`0 1 2 3 4 5 6 7 8 9`

Westbury is a game too do with calculator numbers. First you start with the number 171. The first player has to move 2 matchsticks to make a larger number eg 88 → 1717 and you carry on like this. The loser is when a player cannot make a larger number.

These are all of our sequences.

Vicky started.

| 100 |
| 199 |
| 749 |
| 779 |
| 794 |
| 944 |
| 947 |
| 977 |
| 11911 |
| 114111 |
| 111111 |

Kathy won

Kathy started

| 199 |
| 1194 |
| 11191 |
| 11141 |
| 1111111 |

Kathy won

Vicky started

| 85 |
| 755 |
| 1155 |
| 1164 |
| 1194 |
| 11191 |
| 11141 |
| 1111111 |

Kathy won

Kathy started

| 138 |
| 433 |
| 455 |
| 494 |
| 554 |
| 661 |
| 707 |
| 961 |
| 991 |
| 1491 |
| 1791 |
| 11191 |
| 111141 |
| 1111111 |

Vicky won

This was our longest sequence.

(3) One pattern that I saw was the following: If one player has just changed to this no 111141 they have lost, because the other player changes the no. to 1111111 which is the highest amount that you can get.

Westbury

Equipment: 14 matchsticks.   2 players

Rules:

Numbers on a calculator are all made up from some or all of seven straight lines:

To play *Westbury* you start with the number 88.

The first player must change the positions of exactly two matches to make a bigger number e.g.

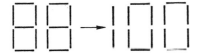

Now the second player must do the same: e.g.

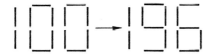

The game continues until a player cannot make a bigger number and loses.

Investigate:

(i)   Play the game. Keep a record of games. How many different sequences can you find? What is the longest?

(ii)   Try starting with other numbers e.g. 60, 180 and see what happens.

Write-up:

(i)   Describe the game in your own words.

(ii)   Make a list of all the sequences you found starting from 88. Which player should win? Can you see any patterns?

(iii)   Give examples of games starting from other numbers and comment on any patterns you notice.

The sixteen game

a/ To play the sixteen game you need two players. A set of cards numbered 0-9 are put face up on the table. Players take turns to pick up a card and the first person to have 3 cards which add up to sixteen is the winner.

b/ Here is a record of a game:-

```
5 |
3 | 2 |     7
9 |         6 8
            4
```

In this case the person who went first won, as they gained an advantage. I don't think it makes a difference to the result who starts, because as long as they take the right card to stop them from getting 16, they can block them.

c/ Here is a list of all the ways 16 can be made:- (with three cards)

```
9999   8888   77     There are 9
7654   785    65       ways.
0123   123    34
```

d/ When you use other target numbers the game is generally the same - as there is only one objective changed. I don't think it's any easier or harder to reach the target.

e/ I think the sixteen game is quite good, because it gets you to think and study what card to take each time. It gets boring, after a while because you just do the same thing over again. It's a good puzzle and makes you think hard and makes your mind work and look at all possibilities.

The Sixteen Game

Equipment: One set of cards numbered 0 to 9.
2 players.

Rules:

At the start of the game all the cards are put face up on the table.

Players take turns to pick up a card. When you choose a card you put it face up in front of you. The winner is the first player to have *three* cards which add up to exactly 16. (If your first three cards do not add up to exactly 16, you continue to choose cards trying to get a set of three totalling 16 exactly.)

Investigate:

(i)   Play some games. Keep a record of some of the games played.

(ii)   What is the best card to choose if you start?

(iii)   In how many ways can you make a total of 16 with three of the cards?

(iv)   Try the game with different target numbers (e.g. 12 or 15) – see what happens.

Write-up:

(i)   Describe the game in your own words.

(ii)   Give a record of a game. Is it better to go first or second?

(iii)   Make a list of all the ways in which you can make 16 with three of the cards.

(iv)   Describe what happens when you use other target numbers.

(v)   What do you think of *The Sixteen Game*?

Manifest

Ten cards 0-9 wrote on then are taken by each player(s)
1 card is placed down by each player then 2,3 x 4. The one with the higest no. winns the points of cards played each turn.

ie. [0]   [2]   player 2 wins gets 1 point.
player 1 player 2

A record of a game played like this.

My points	opponents points
1	0
2	0
0	3
4	0
7	3

The game was then played with cards 0-6. The ways you can pay the game are:

```
with 0-65  65   65
       64  42   64  42
       63  41   63  41
       62  32   62  32
       61  31   61  30
       54  21   60  20
       543      54
       53       53
       52       52
       50       51
       43

      2-65  43
        64  41
        63  40
        61  30
        60  30
        54  10
        53
        51
        50
```

It goes on like this only

The higest total avalible on the 0-9 game is:-

```
10440 = 1
         20
         543  or  5+3
         9876.    9876
```

The lowest score avalible 0-9 game is:

```
3960
   9
  87
 654
3210
```

What I suggest that are the best tactics to use is the 0-9 game are:-

To use a low number 1st eg 0,1,2,3. Then a 4 and 0,1,2,3. which ever left. next 5,0,1,2,3 which is left. then 9876

eg 1, then 40, next 5.321 then 9876.

I liked this best out of Sim & Manifest. It was interesting, fun and enjoyable. I liked it and have enjoyed these lessons.

Manifest

Equipment: Two sets of cards numbered 0 to 9.
Two players.

Rules:

Round 1:   Each player plays one card face down.
When the cards are turned over, the player with the
higher number scores one point. (If numbers are the
same, both players score one point.)
Round 2:   Each player puts two cards face down,
arranged side by side to show the higher value (e.g.
2 and 7 would be used to show 72). When the cards are
turned over, the player with the higher number scores
two points.
Round 3:   Players now play three cards, arranging
them to give the highest number. The winner scores
three points.
Round 4: Players play the last four cards again
arranging for the highest number. The winner scores
four points.

After the fourth round, a new game is started – the
winner is the first player to score 25 points.

Investigate:

(i)   Play a game. See what happens. Now try to
         keep a record of a game played.

(ii)   What do you think is the best number to play
         first?

(iii)   Try the game with just the numbers 0 to 5 and
         see what happens.

Write-up:

(i)   Describe the game in your own words.

(ii)   Give a record of a game played.

(iii)   Make a list of all the possible ways to play the
         0 to 5 game.

(iv)   If you add up all your numbers in the 0 to 9
         game, what are the highest and lowest totals you
         could get?

(v)   Suggest what you think are the best tactics to
         use in the 0 to 9 game.

Investigate

What happens if you use square? With a square it is possible to win but if it is thought throw it is nearly always a draw every time.

Pentagon? The person who goes first usually loses. But its possible to win.

How many lines can you draw if you use:

Square
pentagon
hexagon

Can you find a pattern?

SHAPE	No. of lines
SQUARE	6
PENTAGON	10
HEXAGON	15
HEPTAGON	21
OCTAGON	28
NONAGON	36
DECAGON	45

for 100 dots there would be 4950 lines because because:- $100 \div 2 = -5 \times 100 = 4950$ and it also works with any number. For example:- $7 \div 2 = 3 \cdot 5 - 5 = 3 \times 7 = 21$ or $4 \div 2 = 2 - \cdot 5 = 1 \cdot 5 \times 4 = 6$.

Sim is a good game and tests your eye as well as your brain. And its something to do when your board because someone always wins and its never a draw

Results

Polygon	Total no. of lines
square	6
pentagon	10
Hexagon	15
Heptagon	21
Octagon	28
x.	$\dfrac{x^2 - x}{2}$

As you can see the rule is:- $\dfrac{x^2 - x}{2}$

eg A Pentagon

$5(sides)^2 - 5 \div 2 = 10 \ (25 - 5 = 20 \div 2 = 10)$

An 100 sided shape = 4950

Also the no. of sides on shape + total no of lines = 's the no. of lines on the next shape.

eg Square 4+6=10. 10=no. of lines for pentagon

I thought Sim was good, but after a few games it got a bit boring. I did enjoy it though.

Sim

Equipment: Pencil and paper. 2 players.

Rules:

Six dots are drawn on a piece of paper at the corners of a hexagon:

Players in turn join any two dots with a straight line – each player uses a different colour. You lose if you complete a triangle in your own colour with its corners at points of the hexagon.

Investigate:

(i)   Play some games. Who wins? Keep a record of some games played.

(ii) Try the game starting with (a) a square and (b) a pentagon. What happens?

(iii) How many lines can be drawn with a square, a pentagon, a hexagon . . . can you go on and find a pattern?

(iv) Try a game on a bigger diagram e.g. an octagon

Write-up:

(i)   Describe the game in your own words.

(ii) Give a record of a game you played.

(iii) Describe what happened when you started with a square and a pentagon.

(iv) Make a table showing the number of lines possible for different numbers of sides and describe any patterns you notice.

(v)   If you had time to try a bigger game, describe what happened.

Brussel Sprouts.

crosses at start	no. of lines	winner 1st player or 2nd player
1	3	1st player
2	8	2nd player
3	13	1st player
4	18	2nd player
5	23	1st player
6	28	2nd player

When the number of crosses started with is even the 2nd players win = when the number of crosses started with is odd the first players win.

If a game started with 100 crosses, there would be 498 lines.

Brussel's sprout is quite a good game, but after you have worked it out it is easy to play. It is quite easy to work out.

method = n crosses $(5n - 2)$

Brussels Sprouts

Equipment: Pencil and paper.   Two players.

Rules:

Draw a few crosses on a piece of paper.

Players play alternately. At a turn a player must join the arms of two crosses and put a new cross on the line drawn.

The line drawn can be straight or curved but must not cross other lines or go through other crosses.

The first player who cannot make a move is the loser.

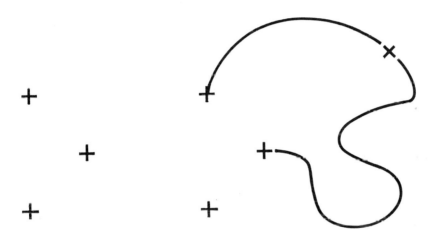

Investigate:

(i)   Play some games. Don't start with too big a number of crosses!

(ii)   Keep a record of a game played.

(iii)   Try the game starting with 2 crosses, then with 3, then 4 and so on. What do you notice?
        Can you see which player will win?

(iv)   Make up a table showing how many lines are drawn in games starting with 2, 3, 4, 5, 6 . . . . crosses. Is there a pattern?
        How many lines would there be for a game starting with 100 crosses?

(v)   What do you think of *Brussels Sprouts?*

Traffic lights

1.

Hayley	Rachel
Y, C	R, C
R, TR	G, C
Y, BL	R, BL
R, TL	G, BL
G, lTL	Y, TL
R, RC	R, BR

KEY
C = Centre
TR = Top right
TL = Top Left
BL = Bottom left
BR = Bottom right
TC = Top centre
BC = Bottom centre
LC = Left centre
RC = Right centre

(I) Hayley made a line of reds, and won.

7 positions left, 2 reds put down.

8 positions left, red changed to yellow.

7 positions left. 2 reds put down.

8 positions left, red changed to yellow.

8 positions left, red changed to yellow.

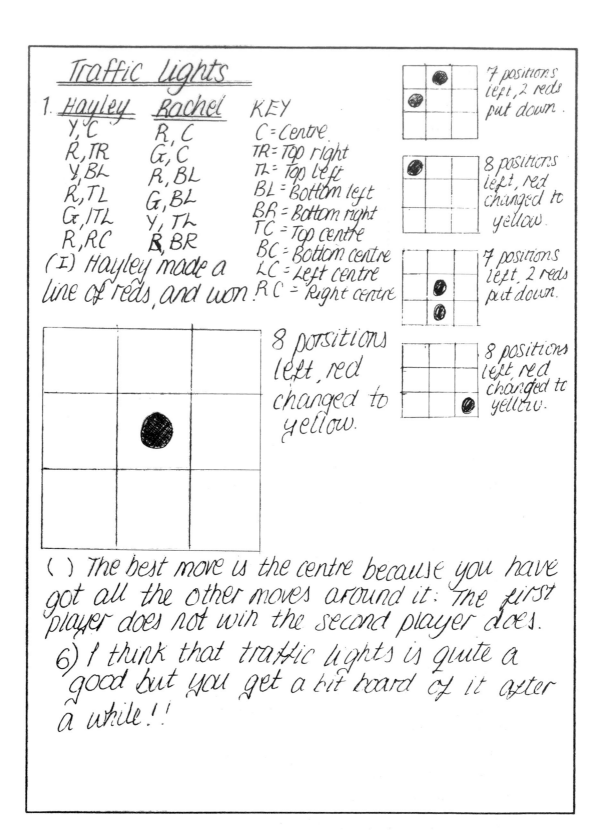

( ) The best move is the centre because you have got all the other moves around it. The first player does not win the second player does.

6) I think that traffic lights is quite a good but you get a bit board of it after a while!!!

Traffic Lights

Equipment: Red, Orange and Green counters.
                2 players.

Rules:

The two players play in turn. At a turn a player can:
either   (i)   put a red counter on an empty square
or   (ii) replace a red counter with an orange one
or   (iii) replace an orange counter with a green one.

The winner is the first player to complete a line in one colour. (The line can be vertical, horizontal or diagonal – as in noughts and crosses.)

Investigate:

(i)   Play some games.

(ii)   Keep a record of a game.

(iii)   How many possible positions are there on the board after one move each? Draw diagrams to show these positions.

(iv)   What is the best move for the player who starts? Should the first player win?

(v)   Try the game on a 4 × 4 board.

(vi)   What do you think of *Traffic Lights*?

Neither the sheets nor the pupils' work are included as 'models': we feel sure that there is scope for improvement in both the posing of the problems and in their solution, but we do hope that the examples given may stir the imagination of teachers and pupils and lead to classroom initiatives.

What do pupils think of games in mathematics lessons? We conclude this chapter with a miscellany of comments:

— Westbury isn't as good as Sim because it isn't like a game and you have to use your brain more.

— I think Sim is a good game for when you are bored.

I think Brussels sprouts is an interesting game but after a few games it becomes boring. I will never play it again unless I can decide whether to go 1st or second.

I quite like Sim. Its good for your maths and enjoyable to play the only thing is it hurts your eyes after a while.

I think it is rather a boring game because of the cube or square numbers pity we could not use normal numbers.

I think games are great. They make Maths lessons more fun and we learn a lot.

- I think Grundys Game is quite boring in a way but also in a way it is quite good. I would recommend it to other people.

- Double or Take is alright for maths but it is not my type of game its prity good considerin we could be doing something a lot harder.

- I don't like Westbury as much as Sim because Westbury is not like a game it is like a test and harder to play.

I think the game Double or Take is a good game. It keeps you awake not like other games like noughts and crosses witch sends you to sleep.

9 GAMES IN THE NATIONAL CURRICULUM

In England and Wales a National Curriculum became compulsory from 1989 for all state schools. The mathematics contained in the curriculum is detailed in *Mathematics in the National Curriculum* (HMSO, 1989). There are two *profile components* for mathematics: the first covers *Number, Algebra and Measures* and the second covers *Shape and Space and Data Handling*. The components are, between them, divided into 14 *Attainment Targets* and 10 *levels* are specified within these targets. School year groups are grouped in 4 *key stages*, stage 1 for 6–7 year olds, stage 2 for 8–11 year olds, stage 3 for 12–14 year olds and stage 4 for pupils of 15 and over.

Where might games find a place in the National Curriculum? As a starting point, it is instructive to look at a list of headings provided in *Mathematics: Non-Statutory Guidance* (National Curriculum Council, 1989); under a section entitled *Schemes of work*. Here it is stated that:

> The overall design and balance of a scheme of work should take into account the following guidelines:

- Activities should bring together different areas of mathematics;

- The order of activities should be flexible;

- Activities should be balanced between tasks which develop knowledge, skills and understanding, and those which develop the ability to tackle practical problems;

- Activities should be balanced between the applications of mathematics and ideas which are purely mathematical;

- Activities should be balanced between those which are short in duration and those which have scope for development over an extended period;

- Activities should, where appropriate, use pupils' own interests or questions either as starting points or as further lines of development;

- Activities should, where appropriate, involve both independent and cooperative work;

- Tasks should be both of the kind which have an exact result or answer and those which have many possible outcomes;

Aren't these things encorporated in maths games such as the number card game?

92

- Activities should be balanced between different modes of learning: doing, observing, talking and listening, discussing with other pupils, reflecting, drafting, reading and writing etc.;

- Activities should encourage pupils to use mental arithmetic and to become confident in the use of a range of mathematical tools;

- Activities should enable pupils to communicate their mathematics;

- Activities should enable pupils to develop their personal qualities;

- Activities should enable pupils to develop a positive attitude to mathematics.

The games and associated activities described in this book would certainly appear to incorporate *all* the points made in these guidelines.

It is difficult to anticipate all the problems which teachers will face as the implementation of the National Curriculum spreads to all levels for 5–16 year olds during the next few years but the busy teacher looking for ideas to enhance a particular curriculum area may find the analysis on page 94 and 95 of some use. We have tried to suggest the particular Attainment Targets for which individual games might provide either useful starting points or helpful enhancement material. However, we would stress that the categorisations are our own and different compilers would almost certainly come up with different classifications. Also, with many games, there are avenues open to exploration which may not be the same as those thought up by the authors of this book but which may well prove exciting and beneficial to pupils. Thus we ask that our 'listing' is used with caution and for rough guidance only and is not interpreted in a manner which is too formal or rigid. Attainment targets 4, 8 and 13 are not included in figure 9.1: we feel that any game contributing to target 3 *necessarily* contributes to target 4 as well, target 8 on *Measures* could easily be incorporated (for example in the construction of equipment), and target 13 is relevant to the investigation of any mathematical situation. Above all we hope that teachers will see the enormous potential of games as activities within the National Curriculum.

The National Curriculum offers considerable opportunities for exciting classroom activity, there is no reason why it should impose great constraints on innovative teaching. A good example of a game and its relevance occurs in a note in *Micromath*, a journal of the Association of Teachers of Mathematics. Margaret Jones (1989) gives details of a computer game called *Digame* which

Suggested suitability of games for the National Curriculum Attainment Targets

Game	Suggested Key Stages	Number/Algebra/Measures						Shape & Space/Handling Data				
		1	2	3	5	6	7	9	10	11	12	14
Chapter 2												
Westbury	1–4	X	X	X	X			X	X	X	X	
Grundy's Game	2–4	X	X	X	X	X					X	
Fair Shares/ Varied Pairs	2–4	X	X	X	X							
Pig	1–4	X	X	X	X			X			X	X
31	2–4	X	X	X	X			X			X	
37	2–4	X	X	X	X			X			X	
57	2–4	X	X	X	X			X			X	
Pentomino Game	1–4	X						X	X	X		
Chapter 3												
Sixteen Game	1–4	X	X	X	X						X	
Nimble	1–4	X	X	X	X						X	
Manifest	1–4	X	X	X	X						X	X
Ten/Twenty	1–4	X	X	X	X						X	
15 Game	1–4	X	X	X	X						X	
Split	2–4	X	X	X	X						X	
Gops	2–4	X	X	X	X						X	
Divide and Conquer	2–4	X	X	X	X						X	
Dirty Dozen	2–4	X	X	X	X						X	X
Chapter 4												
Subtract a Square	2–4	X	X	X	X			X	X		X	
Double or Take	2–4	X	X	X	X						X	
Number Squares	2–4	X	X	X	X						X	
Difference	2–4	X	X	X	X						X	
Undercut	2–4	X	X	X	X						X	X
Division Nim	2–4	X	X	X	X			X			X	X
Takeaway	1–4	X	X	X	X						X	X
Chapter 5												
Three in a Row	1–4	X	X		X			X		X	X	
Sim	2–4	X	X	X	X			X	X	X	X	
Hip	2–4	X	X	X	X	X		X	X	X	X	
Boxes	1–4	X	X					X	X			
Sprouts	2–4	X	X		X	X		X	X	X	X	
Brussels Sprouts	2–4	X	X		X	X		X	X	X	X	

Game	Suggested Key Stages	Number/Algebra/Measures						Shape & Space/Handling Data				
		1	2	3	5	6	7	9	10	11	12	14
Chapter 6												
Next	1–4	X	X		X			X	X	X	X	
Traffic Lights	1–4	X	X	X	X			X	X	X		
Quadromania	2–4	X	X	X	X	X		X	X	X	X	
Black	2–4	X	X					X	X	X	X	
September	3–4	X	X					X	X	X	X	
Continuo	2–4	X	X		X			X	X	X	X	X
Entropy	3–4	X	X	X	X	X		X	X	X	X	
Intersection	3–4	X	X	X	X	X		X	X	X	X	
Chomp	2–4	X	X	X	X			X	X	X	X	
Face Ache	2–4	X	X	X	X			X	X	X	X	
Chapter 7												
Lap	3–4	X					X	X	X	X	X	
Zone X	3–4	X				X	X	X	X	X	X	
Rhino/Elephant	2–4	X	X	X	X	X	X	X	X	X	X	
White Box	3–4	X						X	X	X	X	X
Latino	2–4	X	X	X	X	X		X			X	X
Eleusis	2–4	X	X	X	X	X		X			X	X

(An 'X' in the table indicates that work particularly suited to a target could arise from a game.)

Note: The titles of the Attainment Targets are:

1. Using and applying mathematics
2. Number
3. Number
4. Number
5. Number/Algebra
6. Algebra
7. Algebra
8. Measures
9. Using and applying mathematics
10. Shape and space
11. Shape and space
12. Handling data
13. Handling data
14. Handling data

is a computer version of *Pig* (see chapter 2); the author comments on the reactions and theories of pupils:

for example:

'Every time you get two fives following a one, a one turns up on the next throw.'

'All twos are followed by a one.'

'Two or three high numbers are followed by a one.'

and further observes how appropriate the game was in terms of the National Curriculum quoting, in particular, *Data Handling 1, level 2:*

'Help to design a data collection sheet and use it to record a set of data leading to a frequency table'

One unfortunate consequence of a National Curriculum is the (inevitable) production of lists and tables, such as the list we have devised on pages 94 and 95. It is vital that such lists are not seen as something totally prescriptive and that teachers and pupils should appreciate the need for flexibility in all things. If the content and methods used in mathematics teaching are too tightly defined and perceived then there is the extreme danger of unstimulating and unexciting mathematics classrooms. We hope, particularly, that games may prove to be a vehicle for *discussion* and interaction, one of the inherent dangers in the National Curriculum is that more and more pupils will work *individually* and not have adequate opportunity to talk about mathematics and related activities.

10 COMMENTS ON SELECTED SUGGESTED INVESTIGATIONS

Introductory Note

This chapter includes comments on some of the investigations suggested in the previous chapters. These comments should not be regarded as *solutions* but we hope that they will help to provide some background and, more importantly, further ideas. Many of the investigations do not have *answers*: even where they do, we hope that readers will be encouraged to extend the problems posed and to pursue their own particular lines of enquiry. The greatest satisfaction for all of us (teacher and pupil alike) lies in discovering some new pattern or property at however simple a level. Our notes here may however help the busy teacher to form some idea of possibilities and to gauge some impression of levels to which an investigation might be taken.

Chapter 2: Games with counters, matchsticks and dice

Westbury

(i)   The highest number possible is 1111111. To find other numbers, it may help to consider the number of matches needed to make each digit:

Digit:	0	1	2	3	4	5	6	7	8	9
Matches:	6	2	5	5	4	5	6	4	7	6

Then the possible combinations of 14 matches are:

7+7, 7+5+2, 6+6+2, 6+4+4, 5+5+4, 6+4+4, 6+4+2+2, 6+2+2+2+2, 5+5+2+2, 4+4+4+2, 4+4+2+2+2, 4+2+2+2+2+2, 2+2+2+2+2+2+2.
This leads to 88 (for 7+7), 851, 815, 581, 518, 185, 158, 831, 813, 381, 318, 183, 138, 821, 812, 281, 218, 182, 128 (for 7+5+2) etc.

(ii)   With 2 digits, the highest number is 88.
       With 3 digits, the highest number is 974.

(iv)   With 10 sticks you can make numbers involving: 9, 7; 9, 4;
       9, 1, 1; 7, 6; 7, 0; 7, 7, 1; 7, 4, 1; 6, 4; 6, 1, 1; 4, 4, 1; 5, 3;
       5, 2; 4, 0; 7, 1, 1, 1; 4, 1, 1, 1; 3, 2; 1, 1, 0; 1, 1, 1, 1, 1; 2, 2;
       3, 3; 5, 5. This gives 48 different numbers.

Grundy's Game

(i)   3 counters: player 1 wins
       4 counters: player 2 wins
       5 counters: 4, 1; 3, 1, 1; 2, 1, 1, 1 so player 1 wins
       6 counters: 4, 2; 3, 1, 2; 2, 1, 1, 2 so player 1 wins
       7 counters: player 2 should win
       8 counters: player 1 wins by starting 7, 1
       9 counters: player 1 wins by starting 7, 2
       10 counters: player 2 should win
       11 counters: player 1 wins by starting 10, 1

Fair Shares and Varied Pairs

(i)   With 5 counters you can start with 5, 0; 4, 1; 3, 2.
       5, 0 : player 1 wins by making 1, 1, 1, 1, 1
       4, 1 : player 1 wins by making 1, 1, 1, 1, 1
       3, 2 : if player 1 makes 5, 0 then player 2 wins.
              if player 1 makes 3, 1, 1 then player 2 wins.
              if player 1 makes 1, 1, 1, 2 then player 2 wins.

(iii) Yes for example 5, 0; 3, 2; 5, 0; 3, 2; etc.

Pig

Little comment is possible here since this is largely a data
collecting exercise to be followed by representation and
interpretation.

(v)   This is not an easy calculation. It is probably best to
       calculate the probabilities of finishing with sums from 0 to
       9 first:
       The probability of scoring
       exactly 0 is approximately 16.7%
       exactly 1 is   0
       exactly 2 is approximately 2.8%

exactly 3 is approximately 2.8%
exactly 4 is approximately 3.2%
exactly 5 is approximately 3.7%
exactly 6 is approximately 4.2%
exactly 7 is approximately 2.1%
exactly 8 is approximately 2.8%
exactly 9 is approximately 2.7%

Thus the chance of getting to 10 before throwing a '1' is approximately
$(1 - $ the sum of these probabilities$) = (1-0.41) = 59\%$

The Thirty-one Game

(i) The quickest way of making 31 is in 6 moves for example
$6+6+6+6+5+2$.

    The longest game possible would use:
1, 1, 1, 1, 2, 2, 2, 2, 3, 3, 3, 3, 4, 4, and after these 14 moves, 31 has been exceeded.

(ii) At first sight it looks as though a player should aim to get into the sequence: 3, 10, 17, 24, 31 to win but the real subtlety of the game lies in the fact that it is possible to 'run out' of a particular number.
Player A, if starting, should be able to win by selecting a '5' and then seeking to get into the 10, 17, 24 sequence. If Player B responds with a '5', A should play a '2' and keep answering a '5' with a '2' if necessary. This play would give: 5, 10, 12, 17, 19, 24, 26 and now B must lose.
Even though, at first sight, it appears that it might be best to start with a '3', the sequence: 3, 7, 10, 13, 17, 21, 24, 28 leaves Player A in losing position since there are now no '3s' left!

The Thirty-seven Game

(i) The quickest way to reach 37 is in 9 moves:
5, 4, 5, 4, 5, 4, 5, 4, 1.
The longest way takes 25 moves: 1, 2, 1, 2, ..., 2, 1.

(ii) It is instructive to work backwards. Winning positions are:
36 with '1' covered, 35 with '2', 34 with '3', 33 with '4', 32 with '5'.

The Fifty-seven Game

(i)   There are 4 possible moves from each square. The sums of
      the numbers are:

$$\begin{array}{ccc} 21 & 22 & 17 \\ 16 & 20 & 24 \\ 23 & 18 & 19 \end{array}$$

Notice that each number is 15 more than the original
number in the square. Why?

(ii) The shortest game needs 7 moves: 8, 9, 8, 9, 8, 9, 6.
      The longest game needs 38 moves: 1, 2, 1, 2, ...1, 2.

The Pentomino Game

(i)   Yes, see figure 10.1

(ii) Five, see figure 10.2

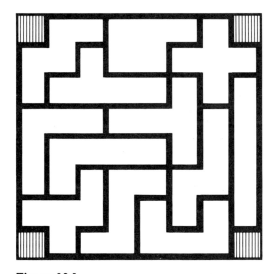

Figure 10.1   **Figure 10.2**

Further interesting properties will be discovered in Golomb (1966).

Chapter 3: Number games with cards

The Sixteen Game

(i)   There are 9 ways. 9+7+0, 9+6+1, 9+5+2, 9+4+3,
        8+7+1, 8+6+2, 8+5+3, 7+6+3,
        7+5+4.

(ii) If you had the 7 cards: 0, 1, 2, 3, 4, 5, 6 you could not use
      three to make 16, in the actual game you could not hold more
      than 5 of these.

(iii) With a pack of cards from 0 to 9:

      Total: 12 13 14 15 16 17 18 19 20 21 22 23
      Ways to
      make: 10 10 10 10 9 8 7 5 4 3 2 1

      Is it possible to predict the number of ways?

(iv) $72 = 2 \times 2 \times 2 \times 3 \times 3 = 2 \times 4 \times 9 = 3 \times 4 \times 6 = 2 \times 3 \times 12 = 1 \times 8 \times 9 = 1 \times 6 \times 12$ so there are five ways of collecting three
      cards with 72 as the product.

Nimble

(i)   You must leave your opponent with 3 cards so that he/she
      can leave only 2 or 1 and you win. To achieve this you
      need to leave 6 cards. Thus the second player can be sure of
      winning if he/she:
      (a) leaves 6 cards on first move (whatever the first player
      does), and
      (b) leaves 3 cards on the next move.

(ii) With 20 cards you need to leave 18, 15, 12, 9, 6, 3 so you
      should start and leave 18 cards after your first move.

(iii) If the rules stipulate 1, 2 or 3 cards and you start with 9
      cards, winning positions are 4 and 8 cards so you should go
      first and take one card.

(iv) With extremely poor play the winner could hold 9, 7, 5, 3, 1
      giving a total of 25.

Manifest

(i) Scores of 9–1, 8–2, 7–3, 6–4, and 5–5 are possible. A player cannot win all four rounds: the best possible win is 9–1, for example

round 1: 0 loses to 8
round 2: 98 beats 97
round 3: 643 beats 642
round 4: 7521 beats 5310

Ten or Twenty

(i) Winning combinations are:
$9+8+3=9+7+4=9+6+5=8+7+5=20$
$7+2+1=6+3+1=5+4+1=5+3+2=10$

(ii) You should select any odd number to win (though '5' is best) for example:

If you start with '5' and your opponent takes an odd number (say '1') then you choose '7' forcing an '8' from your opponent, you take '9' so holdings are now:
You: 5, 7, 9   Opponent: 1, 8, ?
Whatever your opponent takes, you select either 4 or 6 to win;
if you start with '5' and your opponent takes an even number (say '2') then you choose '4' forcing a '1' from your opponent, you take '7' so holdings are now:
You: 5, 4, 7   Opponent: 2, 1, ?
Whatever your opponent takes you select either 8 or 9 to win.

(iii) Yes.

The Fifteen Game

(i) There are 8 possible winning lines:
$9+5+1$, $9+4+2$, $8+6+1$, $8+5+2$, $8+4+3$, $7+6+2$, $7+5+3$, $6+5+4$.

(ii) Yes, for example:

4	5	2
7	1	6
3	8	9

(iii) Only the 'odd' player (with 7, 5, 3 or 9, 5, 1).

Split

(i) All games seem to take 5 or 6 plays, for example:
30;3, 27;3, 4, 23;3, 4, 5, 18;3, 4, 5, 6, 12;3, 4, 5, 6, 1, 11;3, 4, 5, 6, 1, 9, 2
or
30;20, 10;11, 9, 10;11, 9, 6, 4;10, 1, 9, 6, 4;10, 1, 7, 2, 6, 4

(iii) (a) only two games are possible with the cards 1–6: 6;4, 2; 3, 1, 2 or 6;5, 1;2, 3, 1
(b) 14 opening moves are possible. 29, 1; 28, 2; 27, 3; 26, 4; 25, 5; 24, 6; 23, 7; 22, 8; 21, 9; 20, 10; 19, 11; 18, 12; 17, 13; 16, 14.

Gops

(i) The hearts can appear in $6! = 6 \times 5 \times 4 \times 3 \times 2 \times 1 = 720$ ways. One player could win a maximum of 5 of the hearts and the maximum possible score is 20 (6+5+4+3+2). The minimum possible score is 1.

(ii) There are $13! = 6227020800$ possible orders. One player could win a maximum of 12 rounds and score 90 (13+12+11+10+9+8+7+6+5+4+3+2). The minimum possible score is 1.

(iii) For the 13 card game, this is the probability that player two replicates the order for player one viz:
1/13! = 0.0000000001 approx (i.e. very small indeed!).

Divide and Conquer

(i) Card: 2 beats 3, 4, 6, 8, 10, Q
3 beats 4, 6, 9, Q
4 beats 5, 8, Q
5 beats 2, 3, 6, 10
6 beats 4, 7, Q
7 beats 2, 3, 4, 5, 8
8 beats 3, 5, 6, 9
9 beats 2, 4, 5, 6, 7, 10
10 beats 3, 4, 6, 7, 8
Q beats 5, 7, 8, 9, 10

(ii) There are 252 possible combinations possible when selecting 5 cards from 10.

(iii) Yes. For example, using the table above, 2, 3, 4, 5, 6 would beat Q, 9, 8, 10, 7 respectively.

(iv) As an example, with a pack containing the numbers 2 to 14:

	2	3	4	5	6	7	8	9	10	11	12	13	14
2	0	+	+	−	+	−	+	−	+	−	+	−	+
3	−	0	+	−	+	−	−	+	−	−	+	−	−
4	−	−	0	+	−	−	+	−	−	−	+	−	−
5	+	+	−	0	+	−	−	−	+	−	−	−	−
6	−	−	+	−	0	+	−	−	−	−	+	−	−
7	+	+	+	+	−	0	+	−	−	−	−	−	+
8	−	+	−	+	+	−	0	+	−	−	−	−	−
9	+	−	+	+	+	+	−	0	+	−	−	−	−
10	−	+	+	−	+	+	+	−	0	+	−	−	−
11	+	+	+	+	+	+	+	+	−	0	+	−	−
12	−	−	−	+	−	+	+	+	+	−	0	+	−
13	+	+	+	+	+	+	+	+	+	+	−	0	+
14	−	+	+	+	+	−	+	+	+	+	+	−	0

There are some good patterns here. It is also instructive to look at the 'power' of different cards.

The Dirty Dozen

(i)   The quickest route from 20 to 100 is in two moves: +30 followed by 'double your score'.
       The quickest route from −50 to 100 is also in two moves: 'change sign' and 'double your score'.

(ii)   From 0 to 40 in 3 rounds:
       +10, +10, +20 (3 ways); +30, +20, −10 (6 ways); −20, −20, change sign; −10, −30, change sign (2 ways) — giving 12 possible ways.

Chapter 4: Number games with pencil and paper

Subtract a Square

(i)   43 can be written as 36+4+1+1+1 or
36+1+1+1+1+1+1+1 so if player A takes 36 then player
B must leave 6 or 3 and A wins from 6 by taking 4 and
from 3 by taking 1 – so the first player should win.

(ii)/ The numbers from 1 to 50 can all be expressed as the sum
(iv)   of not more than 4 squares. For example 12=9+1+1+1 or
42=36+4+1+1 or 46=36+9+1 etc.
There is a theorem (known as Lagrange's Theorem) that every
positive integer is the sum of four squares, see, for example
Davenport (1952). The reader might also like to refer to Gardner
(1961) and a discussion of *Waring's problem*.
As a variation, the *Eureka* theorem of Gauss states that any
number can be expressed as the sum of not more than three
triangular numbers.

Double or Take

(i)   The crucial number to leave your opponent is a '2' since the
opponent can then only double to 4 (a square) or subtract 1
to leave a square. If A chooses 1, 2, 3, 4, 5, 6, 7, 8, 9, 10
then the winner should be (assuming no silly mistakes)
B, A, B, B, A, B, A, B, B, B (respectively).

(ii)   The numbers 1, 4, 8, 9, 16, 25, 27, 36, 49, 64, 81, 100 give a
win on the next move. The only number which will
guarantee a win after one more move by each player is '2'.

Number Squares

(i)   Yes, a draw is possible for example:

16	6	4	2
3	12	10	8
9	7	5	14
15	13	11	1

(ii)   A draw is not possible. The first player should win by
putting a number other than 1 or 9 in the centre.

Difference

(i)   The maximum possible score is 24. The minimum is 0.
For example:

```
        8   8   7   7   (30)
        1   1   2   2   ( 6)
        3   3   4   4   (14)
        6   6   5   5   (22)
      (18)(18)(18)(18)
```

gives 24 to the row player and 0 to the column player.
The following is an illustration of a 0–0 draw:

```
      8   1   7   2
      1   8   2   7
      3   6   4   5
      6   3   5   4
```

(ii) On an odd sided grid, one square needs to be left blank, the obvious one to choose is the centre square. Thus for a 3×3 square (using the numbers 1 to 4 for each player), the maximum and minimum scores are 9 and 1 for example:

```
      4   3   4   (11)
      1   —   1   ( 2)
      2   3   2   ( 7)
     (7) (6) (7)
```

(iii) With a single set of numbers from 1 to 16, the maximum score is 48 [(16+15+14+13) − (4+3+2+1)] and the minimum score is 0 [for example: (16+8+6+1) − (15+9+5+2)]. There are interesting links here with magic squares, see Ball and Coxeter (1974).

Undercut

(i)   There are 25 ways.

(ii) The quickest game is three moves for example (4, 5), (4, 5), (4, 5) in which the first player would score 27.
      The longest game would take 25 moves. Since a minimum of 2 points must be scored in each round, after 25 rounds both players must have reached/exceeded the target of 25.

It is interesting to analyse in terms of your score in relation to your opponent's:

		Opponent				
		1	2	3	4	5
	1	0	+3	−2	−3	−4
	2	−3	0	+5	−2	−3
You	3	+2	−5	0	+7	−2
	4	+3	+2	−7	0	+9
	5	+4	+3	+2	−9	0

The table shows your gain for any pair of scores. Some good patterns emerge as well as some pointers to possible strategies!

Division Nim

(ii) $36 = 2 \times 2 \times 3 \times 3 = 2 \times 2 \times 9 = 2 \times 3 \times 6 = 3 \times 3 \times 4 = 3 \times 12$

This gives five games (with different orders possible). If the first player divides by 12, the second player is left with 3 and loses.

Takeaway

(i) Since the numbers 1 to 16 have the sum 136, a score of 69 or more will win for example $16 + 15 + 14 + 13 + 12 = 70$ would give a win in 5 plays.

(ii) A draw is possible with a score of 68 for each player for example $16 + 14 + 12 + 9 + 7 + 5 + 3 + 2$ and $15 + 13 + 11 + 10 + 8 + 6 + 4 + 1$. Other draws are also possible when some cards become inaccessible.

Chapter 5: Geometrical games with pencil and paper

Three in a row

(i) The first player can win by placing a cross on the middle dot and then following every move of the second player with a symmetrical move, until the opportunity to make three crosses together occurs.

(ii) With an odd number of dots (at least five), the above strategy will always guarantee a win.

With an even number the first player will win with 4 dots, the second player with 6 dots, the first player with 8 dots (by starting at an end) and the first player with 10 dots. Is there a pattern?

Sim

(i) With both a square and a pentagon a draw normally occurs.

(ii) The table shows the number of lines which can be drawn for different numbers of points at the start.

No of sides:	3	4	5	6	7	8	9	...
No of lines:	3	6	10	15	21	28	36	...

There are some good patterns to spot here. If a game starts with n points, then $[n(n-1)/2]$ lines are possible (compare with triangular numbers).

(iii) Using just the original points as vertices 20 triangles are possible, 10 are isosceles and 10 are right-angled.

(iv) 3. You can join a point to a neighbouring one, or a neighbour +1, or a neighbour +2.

(v) No. No one seems to have found one!

Hip

(ii) For a 6×6 dot grid, 105 squares are possible.
The pattern is as follows:

Grid size:	2×2	3×3	4×4	5×5	6×6	7×7
Squares:	1	6	20	50	105	196

In general, for an n×n grid, there are $[n^2(n^2-1)/12]$ squares possible (see also chapter 8).

Boxes and variations

(i) With 4 dots, player 2 wins. With 6 dots, player 1 should win if they start as indicated.

(ii) The longest worm seems to be one of 63 units (go down an edge, one unit along the bottom, up to top again, along one unit, down to bottom and so on).

(iii) 12×90 = 1080 degrees.

Sprouts

(i) With 1 dot: a maximum of 2 moves is possible, with 2 dots: a maximum of 5 moves.

(ii) The number of moves for a game with n dots at the start must lie between $2n$ and $(3n-1)$.

Brussels Sprouts

(ii)

Crosses at start:	1	2	3	4	5	6	....
No of moves:	3	8	13	18	23	28	....

For n crosses there will be $(5n-2)$ moves.

(iii) If you start with an even number of crosses, player 2 will win; if you start with an odd number then player 1 wins. Thus the result of the game is predetermined and no skill whatsoever is involved!

Chapter 6: Geometrical games with boards

Next

(i)   If at the start the first counter goes in space '1', there are 8 ways of placing a second counter of a different colour and 5 ways of placing one of the same colour.

   With three counters to be placed (the first to go in space '1'), there are 28 ways of placing them if they are all different colours, 4 ways if they are all the same colour (first in '1' then 4, 7; 4, 8; 4, 9 and 5, 8 are possible placings).

(ii)   The smallest number of counters which can be placed before further placing is impossible is 6.
   (For example colour 'A' in spaces 1,7; colour 'B' in spaces 4, 8 and colour 'C' in spaces 2, 9.)

Traffic Lights

(i)   After one move by each player there will be either 2 reds on the board (8 distinct possible ways) or 1 orange (3 ways) so there are 11 possible positions after one move by each player.

(ii)   Five.

(iii)   Three moves for the shortest game. For the longest, a line must exist after 24 moves.

(iv)   No.

Quadromania

(i) The highest possible score is 42. (For example 4×10 for four colour quads in each quadrant and 1×2 for a centre quad of four different colours).
The lowest possible score is zero.

(ii) Yes.

(iii) There are 9 possible quads and 10 possible rows.

(iv) Yes. 0 – 0 is possible and also other scores for example 14 – 14.

Black

The number of ways in each case will be large!

September

(i) The shortest possible path is 6 units (using 6 'straights').
The longest possible path is 13 units (using all the pieces and including some doubling back).
    There are 6 ways of getting across using 7 'straights' and 1 way using 6.

        5 'straights' and 1 'L' give   6×2=12 ways
        4 straights and 2 'L' give   15×4=60 ways
        3 straights and 3 'L' give   20×8=160 ways

giving a total of 239 ways if no doubling back is included. There are plenty of further ways to find if doubling back is included!

(ii) Yes.

Continuo

When the game was first introduced, a prize of £1000 was offered for the arrangement of the cards giving the highest possible score. We do not know the answer!

Entropy

(i) On a 2×2 board the maximum possible score is 4.

On a 3×3 board the maximum possible score
is 21.
On a 4×4 board the maximum possible score is 64.
In general, on an n×n board, the maximum possible score
is [$n^2(n-1)(n+4)/6$]. (See also chapter 8)

(ii) Yes.

Intersection

(i) The shortest possible game will end after 9 counters have
been taken for example, see figure 10.3.
     Row player to 'A', column player to '1' and takes A1.
Thereafter counters are taken at: E1, E2, D2, D1, C1, C2,
B2, B1 and the game ends.
     The longest possible game involves 21 counters being
taken for example A1, E1, E2, B2, B4, D4, D5, A5, A3, C3,
C1, B1, B5, E5, E3, D3, D2, A2, A4, C4, C2.

(ii) The minimum possible score is 4.
     The maximum possible score is 76, for example if a
player captured 7 black and 4 blue counters, the score
would be (2×28 + 2×10). (Remember that your score is
doubled if you hold a colour which is not held by your
opponent.)

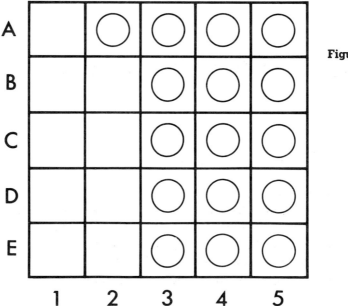

Figure 10.3

Face Ache

(i) 3. Two possible squares and one rectangle. (Assuming rotations of the board are regarded as the same.)

(ii) 3×3: 3 distinct positions
4×4: 3 distinct positions
5×5: 6 distinct positions (See figure 10.4).

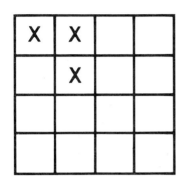

Figure 10.4

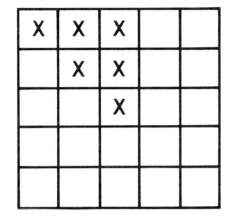

(iii) There are 2 positions on a 2×3 rectangle and 6 on a 3×5 rectangle.

Chomp

(ii) On a 3×3 grid the longest game involves 8 moves and the shortest involves 2 moves before the poison counter must be taken.

Chapter 5: Inferential Games

Lap

(i) Some examples are given in figure 10.5.

(iv) You can use any n×n grid if n is even.
    If *n* is odd, you could leave the centre square blank (for example on a 5×5 grid you would use 24 squares). For a square which is (2n−1) by (2n−1), since $(2n-1)(2n-1) = 4(n^2-n) + 1$, it will always be possible to divide the board into four equal regions with one square left empty.

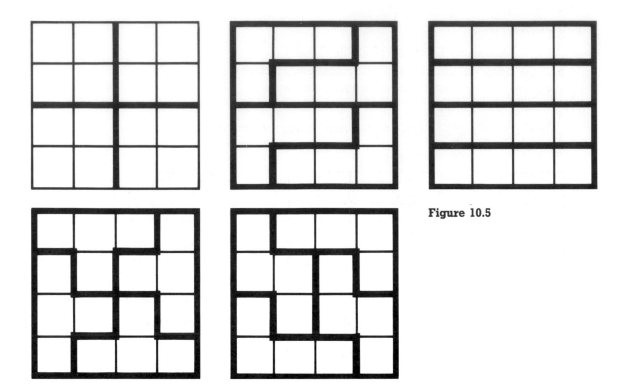

Figure 10.5

Zone X

(i) A minimum of three questions is needed to identify a straight line (two are not enough because the points might belong to different lines).

(ii) Three lines will create 7 regions in general, 6 if the lines are concurrent.

In general:

Lines:	2	3	4	5	6	... n
Max no of regions:	4	7	11	16	22	... $(n^2+n+2)/2$

Rhino and Elephant

(i) In *Rhino*:

Answer:	1	2	3	4	... n
Possible points:	4	8	12	16	... 4n

In *Elephant*

Answer:	1.414	2.236	2.828	3.162	...
Possible points:	4	8	4	8	...

(some good diagrams can be produced here, for example figure 10.6).

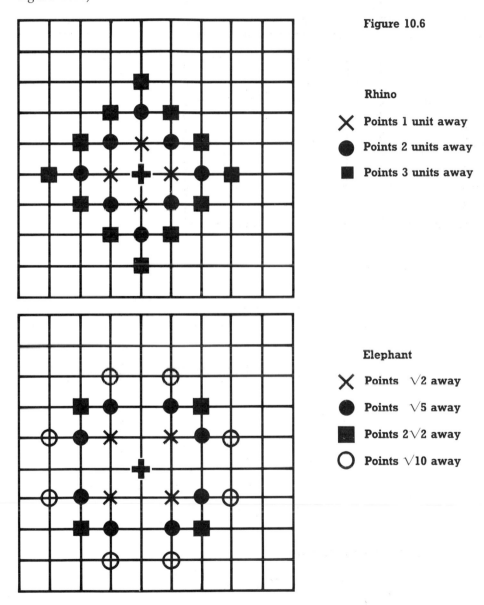

Figure 10.6

Rhino

✗ **Points 1 unit away**

● **Points 2 units away**

■ **Points 3 units away**

Elephant

✗ **Points √2 away**

● **Points √5 away**

■ **Points 2√2 away**

○ **Points √10 away**

(ii) In *Elephant* three is the smallest number of questions required because after two questions there are two positions possible.

In *Rhino*, three is normally the smallest number of questions although two will sometimes suffice.

White Box

(i) With one mirror, there are 3 available faces wherever it is put. Therefore a ray coming from any direction along the appropriate row will strike the mirror and the position will then be identifiable. For example, in figure 10.7
if the rays are injected at A, B, C, D, E, F the mirror will be found in at most *six* attempts.

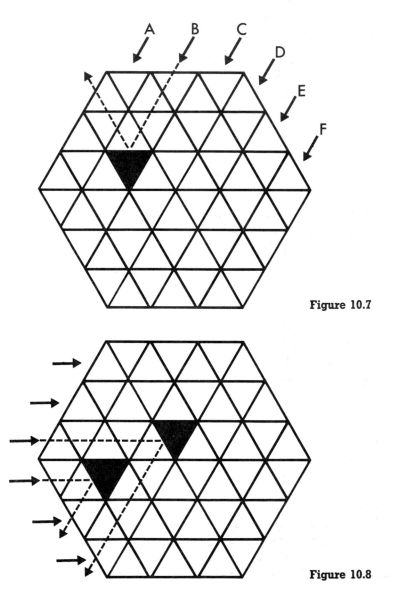

Figure 10.7

Figure 10.8

(ii) With two mirrors:
  (a) if the mirrors are in different rows, 6 rays are needed (see figure 10.8).
  (b) if the mirrors are in the same row but not touching, it depends on initial choice of direction for the rays. In figure 10.9(a) and (b), 6 rays are needed but in figure 10.9(c), 7 rays are needed.
  (c) if the mirrors are in the same row and touching, then a minimum of 7 rays is needed (see figure 10.10).

Thus in general, for 2 mirrors, 7 rays should always be sufficient. With *three* mirrors, the worst possible case is when they are all in the same row when a maximum of 12 rays may be needed.

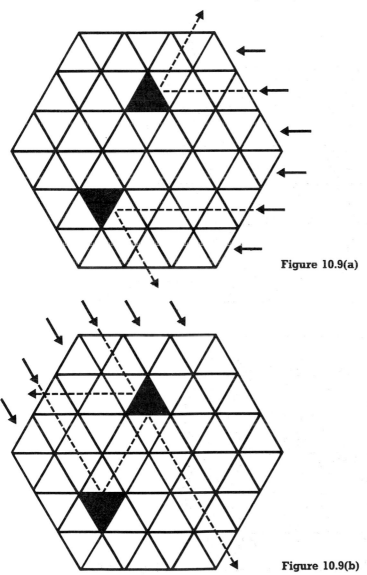

Figure 10.9(a)

Figure 10.9(b)

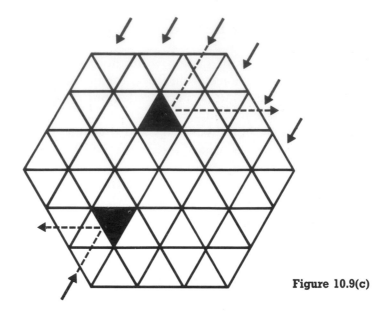

Figure 10.9(c)

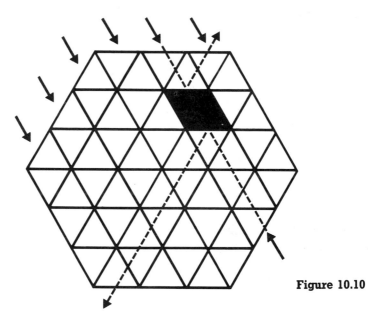

Figure 10.10

118

Latino

(i) Yes, for example:

```
1  2        3  1  2        2  3  4  1
2  1        2  3  1        3  4  1  2
            1  2  3        4  1  2  3
                           1  2  3  4
```

```
1  2  3  4  5
2  3  4  5  1
3  4  5  1  2
4  5  1  2  3
5  1  2  3  4
```

There are some interesting patterns to explore here.

(ii)

Size	2×2	3×3	4×4	5×5 ...
Row/Column Total	3	6	10	15 ...

(iii)

	A	B	C	D	E	F
6	2	6	1	3	5	4
5	6	1	2	4	3	5
4	5	3	4	6	2	1
3	4	2	5	1	6	3
2	1	5	3	2	4	6
1	3	4	6	5	1	2

(iv) On an 8×8 grid, with pairs totals of 3, 4, 5,...15 are possible, with trios totals of 6, 7, 8,...21 are possible.

Eleusis

(ii) 8. (four 2s and 4 9s)

(iii) If the last card is a 7 then there are 24 possible 'right' plays – 3, 5, 6, 8, 10, Q of each suit.
Rules are often difficult to guess. One class of 11 year olds was baffled for days by a game. The rule setter eventually disclosed that the rule was for the names of the numbers to be in alphabetical order, in French!

BIBLIOGRAPHY AND SUGGESTED READING

For a generation or more the outstanding name in all aspects of recreational mathematics has been Martin Gardner. Several collections of his writings are available, many of them in paperback editions, some, which include games similar to those featured in this book, are given below.

In the world of games Sid Sackson is as pre-eminent as Martin Gardner in recreational mathematics. His *A Gamut of Games* is probably the book the aficionado would rescue before all others should his house catch fire!

Five-Minute Games, by David Pritchard, is a collection of little-known and unusual games. Unfortunately, like many other valuable sources, it is currently out of print, although copies may be obtainable through libraries. The same remarks apply to David Silverman's *Your Move*.

A good general games collection is *The Indoor Games Book* by Andrew Pennycook.

Mathematics in School, a journal of the Mathematical Association (published by Longman), devoted a special issue to mathematical games in January, 1986 and between 1986 and 1989 included a series of 12 articles entitled *Maths Games Workshop* by David Kirkby, see, for example, the March 1988 issue.

Books by the present writers include *Board Games Round the World* by Robbie Bell and Michael Cornelius (which is also available in German and Spanish editions) and *Take Ten Cards* by Alan Parr.

Bibliography

Abbott, R. (1963) *Abbott's New Card Games*, Funk and Wagnalls
Abbott, R. (1977) *The New Eleusis*, Robert Abbott, New York
Ault, L.H. (1976) *The Official Mastermind Handbook*, New English Library
Ault, L. H. (1978) *The Official Mastermind Puzzle Book*, Signet, New American Library
Averbach, B. and Chein, D. (1980) *Mathematics: Problem Solving Through Recreational Mathematics*, Freeman
Ball, W.W. and Coxeter, H.S.M. (1974) *Mathematical Recreations and Essays*, University of Toronto Press
Bell, R. and Cornelius, M. (1988) *Board Games Round the World*, Cambridge University Press

Bolt, B. (1982) *Mathematical Activities*, Cambridge University Press

Courant, R. and Robbins, H. (1969) *What is Mathematics?*, Oxford University Press

Davenport, H. (1952) *The Higher Arithmetic*, Hutchinson

Deft, J. (1987) *Mathematics Games*, Macmillan

Dudeney, H. (1958) *The Canterbury Puzzles*, Dover Publications

Gardner, M. (1961) *The Second Scientific American Book of Puzzles and Diversions*, Simon and Schuster

Gardner, M. (1971) *More Mathematical Puzzles and Diversions*, Pelican.

Gardner, M. (1973) 'Mathematical Games' in *Scientific American*, January, 1973

Golomb, S.W. (1966) *Polyominoes*, Allen and Unwin

HMSO, (1989) *Mathematics in the National Curriculum*, HMSO/DES

Jones, Margaret (1989) 'Digame' in *Micromath*, Vol 5 No 2, Association of Teachers of Mathematics

Kirkby, D. et al (1984) *Maths Games in the Classroom*, Eigen Publications

Kohl, H.R. (1974) *Writing Maths and Games in the Open Classroom*, Methuen

Mathematical Association (1986) Special edition of *Mathematics in School*, Longman

National Curriculum Council, (1989) *Mathematics; Non Statutory Guidance*, National Curriculum Council

Parr, A. (1991) *Take Ten Cards*, Egon Publications

Pennycook, A. (1973) *The Indoor Games Book*, Faber and Faber

Polya, G. (1957) *How to Solve It*, Doubleday Anchor Books

Pritchard, D. (1984) *Five-Minute Games*, Bell and Hyman

Robin, A.C. (1989) 'Problem Corner' in *Mathematical Gazette*, Vol 73, No 466

Sackson, S. (1969) *A Gamut of Games*, Random House

Silverman, D.L. (1971) *Your Move*, Kaye and Ward

Simmons, G.J. (1969) 'The Game of Sim' in *Journal of Recreational Mathematics*, Vol 2, April 1969

Tapson, F. (1986) 'Maths Resource' in *Mathematics in School*, Vol 15 No 1, January, 1986

Truran, T. (1984) *Masterful Mindbenders*, Octopus Books

Waddington (1983) *Waddington's Illustrated Card Games*, Pan Books

Some sources for computer software

Versions (for BBC series computers) of *the 31 game*, *the 37 game* and *the 57 game* can be found among eight games included in *Anita Straker Number Games* available from ESM, Duke Street, Wisbech, Cambs PE13 2AE. Another ESM collection *Maths 9–13* includes several more games including *Rollers*, a version of *Pig*.

An alternative version of *Pig*, called *Digame*, can be found on SLIMWAM2 available from the Association of Teachers of Mathematics, 7 Shaftesbury Street, Derby, DE3 8YB.

Elephant, *Rhino* and a simple form of *Mastermind* are all included in *The First 30*, a collection of games, puzzles and investigations in the *Microsmile* series which was originally produced by ILEA.

Black Box can be found in the *MEP Problems and Investigations* collection. This set includes a number of other games including a version of *Sim*. Local computer advisory centres should be able to provide copies.

Unfortunately, computer versions of most of the games in this book do not, at present, exist even though the games themselves offer an ideal project to those with programming skills. The authors would be delighted to hear about computer versions of *Subtract a Square*, *Latino*, *Traffic Lights* or any of the many other games in this book.

Index